"Accessible and engaging, personalizes ancient women ᴛʜʀᴏᴜɢʜ ᴄʟᴏꜱᴇ ᴀɴᴅ imaginative readings of historical texts, including significant portions of the New Testament. She both models this method and gives students all the resources they need to do it on their own. By challenging the assumption that 'women weren't able to do much,' *Finding Phoebe* has the potential to dislodge a stale debate over women in society and the church then and now."

—REV. DR. AMY PEELER
Wheaton College

"A welcome correction to stereotyping of ancient Mediterranean women as passive and helpless, this is a very readable portrayal of what we know about women leaders with social power, both in the world around them and for the people of the New Testament. Hylen draws on multiple real examples from inscriptions and ancient texts to place familiar biblical texts in proper context and navigates the conflicting images and seemingly contrary evidence about women of the New Testament world."

—DR. CAROLYN OSIEK
Brite Divinity School

"It may well seem to some that Phoebe, who is praised by Paul in Romans 16:1–2, appears out of thin air. More thorough investigation reveals, however, that she was not a solitary female figure—neither in Romans 16, nor in other Pauline letters, nor in the New Testament and its fascinating world. In her instructive, insightful, innovative, and interactive volume *Finding Phoebe*, Susan E. Hylen helps nonspecialists understand Phoebe—and other women of her time and ilk—more fully by exploring the complex, variegated socio-historical milieu in which they lived and moved and had their being. . . . This volume will inform, if not transform, the way you perceive women in the New Testament and its environs in general and in Paul and his letters in particular."

—DR. TODD STILL
Baylor University

"Prepare to question some of your basic assumptions! In this delightfully engaging book, Hylen leads us on an active learning journey that involves visiting both new evidence and old in order to reconsider our cherished (but perhaps outdated or misguided) certitudes about New Testament women. . . . Ever the careful, keen, logical New Testament scholar who neither over- nor understates the case, in this book Hylen also displays her teaching prowess. Each chapter leads with some noteworthy aspect of Phoebe, then draws us into imagining life on the ground in the first-century world (using a fictional Roman family to flesh out the main ideas in a concrete way), and then applies what has just been discussed to exercises centered on New Testament texts (so, yes, there is homework, but of the best sort!). Hylen knows what questions we the readers have, especially those of us for whom the New Testament is Scripture. . . . I will certainly recommend this book both for individual and group study. I was so interested that I read it all in one sitting because each chapter is just the right length to make you want to read the next one promptly!"

—REV. DR. JAIME CLARK-SOLES
Southern Methodist University

"Paul's respect and admiration for Phoebe, named in Romans 16, is evident. But with only two short verses describing her, what can be said about this woman? Hylen's *Finding Phoebe* is a rich and readable examination of historical examples of women functioning as patrons, benefactors, property owners, industrial workers, and those who wielded robust social involvement and power. The carefully crafted study questions based on primary sources are a great way for students to discover the various roles women played in antiquity. By the end of Hylen's study, readers will have a much more informed account of who Phoebe was and the cooperative role she played in Paul's mission."

—DR. JOSHUA W. JIPP
Trinity Evangelical Divinity School

Finding Phoebe

What New Testament Women Were Really Like

SUSAN E. HYLEN

WILLIAM B. EERDMANS PUBLISHING COMPANY
GRAND RAPIDS, MICHIGAN

Wm. B. Eerdmans Publishing Co.
4035 Park East Court SE, Grand Rapids, Michigan 49546
www.eerdmans.com

Published 2023
Printed in the United States of America

29 28 27 26 25 24 23   2 3 4 5 6 7

ISBN 978-0-8028-8206-6

Library of Congress Cataloging-in-Publication Data

A catalog record for this book is available from the Library of Congress.

For Jen

Contents

Acknowledgments

I am grateful to many people for the assistance I had in writing this book. The initial phases of writing were made possible by a sabbatical leave from Candler School of Theology and through a Teacher-Scholar Grant from the Calvin Institute of Christian Worship, Grand Rapids, Michigan, with funds provided by Lilly Endowment Inc. The final stages of writing and revision were further supported by a manuscript completion grant from Candler School of Theology. I am grateful to the Calvin Institute and the deans at Candler for their generous support.

A number of collaborators also helped me consider how to make this book useful to a wider audience. April McGee, Kimber Wiseman, and Amber Byers read an early draft of the project. I had further conversations with Daniel Vestal, Ike Reeser, Pam Purso, Don McLaughlin, Raushanah Butler, and Elizabeth Rogers about their experiences talking with churches about women in ministry. I am so thankful for their time commitment and willingness to share their wisdom. Margot Starbuck and Ulrike Guthrie provided invaluable advice and editorial assistance, and Anne Richardson offered many good ideas for the cover.

I am also thankful for the many relationships that have sustained me through the rather long process of conceiving and writing this rather short book. Before our sabbaticals were disrupted by the pandemic, I shared many lunches with Beth Corrie and Alison Greene. I am grateful to them—and to Jen Ayres, Ellen Ott Marshall, and Arun Jones—for taking time from the busyness of academic life to tend the bonds of collegiality.

My family keeps me going through the daily challenges of writing. Ted Smith somehow inspires everyone around him to do better work than they knew was possible. Thank you for being my partner in everything and my trusted friend. Our sons, Bennett and Tobias, keep me grounded and add meaning to all that I do.

This book is dedicated in memory of Jennifer Wegter-McNelly, the best pastor I have ever known. Her creativity, dedication to ministry, and no-nonsense perseverance have always inspired and encouraged me. I am grateful to have been among her friends.

Introduction

Two tantalizing verses at the end of Romans raise many questions about women's roles in the earliest churches. There, Paul writes, "I commend to you our sister Phoebe, a deacon of the church in Cenchreae. I ask you to receive her in the Lord in a way worthy of his people and to give her any help she may need from you, for she has been the benefactor of many people, including me" (Rom. 16:1–2).[1] He calls Phoebe "sister," "deacon," and "benefactor," and he commends her to the church in Rome.

Who was Phoebe, and what did she do? What was involved in being a deacon or benefactor? She obviously traveled a long way, from Cenchreae (near Corinth in Greece) to Rome. And she is sufficiently important for Paul to include her in his letter. But these two verses are the only time she's mentioned. What sort of role did Phoebe have, either at her home church or during her travels to Rome? Wouldn't it be interesting to know more about her?

Interpreters differ in understanding Phoebe's role in the church. Some suggest that she was an early church leader—ordained as a deacon, a patron of Paul and others in the church. Others argue that she had only an informal role in serving Paul—she was a helper but not a minister of the gospel.

These arguments about Phoebe reflect larger debates among Christians today about how to understand the roles of women in the New

Testament. After Phoebe, Paul mentions a number of other women, women like Prisca, Mary, and Junia (Rom. 16:3–4, 6, 7). Though Paul describes them in different ways, they all seem to have had some kind of role in spreading the gospel. Women also played a variety of roles in the Gospels and Acts. But then, as if to contradict this, a number of passages direct women to be silent or subordinate to men. As with Phoebe, there are a wide variety of interpretations of each of these texts.

Yet passages like these play an important role in arguments for and against women's leadership in churches today, and Christians turn to the Bible and such passages for answers. They ask whether women in the time of Jesus or Paul played the kinds of roles we now assign to ministers or whether women held church offices. They look for clues to how God views human gender differences.

How do we decide? When we interpret the verses about Phoebe, for example, we make a whole lot of decisions about what the text means, often without really noticing ourselves doing so. We decide what it means that Paul calls Phoebe a "deacon" and a "benefactor." We think about what it meant for the Romans to "receive" her and to "give her any help she may need." We may consider the context of the letter in which these verses appear, or wonder about the ancient context: Were Paul's words here a standard practice of ancient letter writing? All of these things can help us understand Phoebe.

The basic idea is that women weren't able to do much.

As we read the New Testament, we often try to re-create some of the knowledge that ancient readers had, in order to understand it in the way they would have. Although the New Testament still speaks to people today as Scripture, understanding its meaning often involves studying the historical context of the first century. Presumably, the first recipients of Paul's letter understood what he meant by "commending" Phoebe. They drew on shared cultural knowledge to make sense of his words. They knew what a "deacon" was back then, and what a "benefactor" did. They knew something about the practice of introducing a traveler to a new city, and they knew whether it was common or unusual for women to have leadership roles, either in churches or anywhere else in their society. Paul's first readers brought all that information with them to the letter. We can only try to re-create some of what they knew.

Interpreters today often share a picture of women's lives in the New Testament period, which they draw on to interpret passages like this. The basic idea is that women weren't able to do much. Women were subject to men and unable to wield real authority. They did not own property or participate in civic life in significant ways. They were not educated. Although a few interpreters suggest that some women were acting contrary to this, they usually agree that this behavior was unusual or new. Social conditions created opportunities for some (usually elite) women to exercise power, but this was not conventional, and the behavior often attracted criticism.

My research into the history of the New Testament contradicts many of these assumptions about women. I want to paint a more accurate picture of women's lives, roles, and abilities for you. The main differences are:

- Women owned property and exercised authority over their affairs.
- Like other property owners, women served as patrons, using their wealth and social influence to support civic and religious causes.
- Though the culture deemed women to be inferior to men, nonetheless women participated in community life, including in leadership roles. People at the time did not see this as contradictory, and indeed the tension was part of the social fabric.

If you think information like this would be useful for understanding the New Testament, this book is for you.

Having more historical information won't answer every one of our questions or solve every difficulty we have interpreting a passage of Scripture. We won't know what Phoebe did on her visit to Rome, or how long she stayed. We won't know if she was married, or what she did for a living. There are limits to what we can know about individual women like Phoebe.

Having a new view of women in history is not likely to spark widespread agreement about how to interpret New Testament texts that mention women—let alone about the roles women should play in churches today. After all, until now we've agreed that ancient women's lives were highly restricted, and that did not cause widespread agreement on particular passages or on questions of women's leadership. It seems unlikely that a new history will change our varied opinions on the matter. However, because many readers of the New Testament want to understand the ancient context, it seems appropriate to consider the most recent historical evidence available.

It seems unlikely that a new history will change our varied opinions on the matter.

This book sets out that evidence in an accessible way for people who care about these questions. If you find yourself wanting more in-depth history, I have written a more detailed book, intended for college or seminary audiences (Susan E. Hylen, *Women in the New Testament World* [Oxford University Press, 2018]). But lots of people outside of classrooms are also interested in this subject, and this book is for anyone with an interest in the topic. It lays out ancient evidence and then asks you to consider New Testament passages in light of that historical context. The evidence provided here is representative rather than exhaustive.

Each chapter takes up one aspect of women's lives in the New Testament period. To narrow the focus in a way that's most relevant for us, we'll only consider evidence from the first century BCE through the second century CE. The chapters in part 1 explore patterns of wealth and legal norms around property rights. Part 2 discusses social influence and status. Part 3 addresses the traditional virtues that women were expected to exhibit. To modern readers, traditional virtues like modesty seem to contradict the behavior of women seen in parts 1 and 2, so these chapters explain how ancient people may have understood them to be compatible. Part 4 addresses women's speech and social expectations of silence. The conclusion helps you integrate the pieces and decide how it matters to you.

Each chapter ends with some New Testament texts for you to consider. Though I will often discuss one or two passages as examples, rather than give you an "answer" to each passage, my intention is more to help you think about the historical background and then interpret the New Testament yourself. The instructions are designed to help you think about them as if you were an ancient reader who was shaped by the cultural expectations of the time. Each chapter will describe the social background, and it's your job to imagine yourself as a reader who is shaped by those conventions.

Imagining the Lives of Ancient Women

Understanding the perspectives of ancient readers of the Bible isn't easy. One reason is that, even after all these years, there is still quite a lot of evidence available and many different kinds of it—literary works, inscriptions, and fragments of paper with everyday items like receipts. Each gives us a different type of information about ancient life. But even with all that evidence, our picture remains fragmentary, and we have to piece it together from all these various sources.

Another reason it's hard to understand ancient perspectives is that we are so embedded in our own modern perspectives. Most people have ideas about what the lives of women in antiquity were like. But by being so sure those ideas are right we sometimes miss evidence to the contrary because we're already sure it doesn't exist. So we have to try to set aside all of our assumptions about what women did or did not do in order to consider the evidence.

History requires an act of imagination.

History requires an act of imagination. That might seem surprising if you learned history in a way that mostly entailed memorizing names and dates. But when we think historically, we try to imagine what life was like in a culture (and time and place) very different from our own. The task is not simply to be open-minded in a general sense, but to try to imagine, on the basis of the evidence that we have, how ancient people organized their lives.

To get you started thinking about ancient women in a new way, try to forget everything you know (or think you know, or have heard) about women in the ancient world and consider one piece of evidence: this inscription from first-century Cartima (a city in Roman Spain). What conclusions about ancient women can you draw from this one piece of writing?

> Junia Rustica, daughter of Decimus, first and perpetual priestess in the city of Cartima, restored the public porticos that had decayed due to old age, gave land for a bathhouse, reimbursed the public taxes, set up a bronze statue of Mars in the forum, gave at her own cost porticos next to the bathhouse on her own land, with a pool and a statue of Cupid, and dedicated them after giving a feast and public shows. Having remitted the expense, she made and dedicated the statues that were decreed by the council of Cartima for herself and her son, Gaius Fabius Junianus, and she likewise made and dedicated at her own cost the statue for Gaius Fabius Fabianus, her husband.[2]

Now:

1. List all the active verbs that record Junia's actions—that is, what she does (I've supplied the first two verbs as an example):

"restored"

"gave"

2. List the phrases in the inscription that describe her ownership of wealth:

3. List the phrases in the inscription that suggest her civic involvement:

4. If you find anything surprising in the piece of writing, or anything that contradicts your ideas about ancient women, name those new things and what you previously thought. That way, you can test those ideas as you encounter more evidence. (After all, the idea is not to draw historical conclusions on the basis of one piece of evidence . . . this is just an exercise to get your imagination going!) At the end of the book, I'll remind you to come back and see what else you discovered that might speak to your questions.

*

If the inscription honoring Junia Rustica was the only one of its kind, this exercise wouldn't be very helpful. But it was not the only one— not by a long shot. It turns out there were a lot of women like Junia Rustica in the first and second centuries CE. I give a few more specific examples in the chapters that follow, but there are many more. It's true that men appear more frequently than women in inscriptions like this, but there are enough women that we need to consider this evidence and think about the social and legal structures that made it possible. The chapters that follow describe some of the reasons why women of this time period were able to do the kinds of things Junia Rustica did. Some of this evidence is "new" in the sense that, although it has existed for two thousand years, scholars have only recently made it available to us to consider. Now that more evidence is available, we should reconsider some of the conclusions we've drawn in the past. As we sort through the evidence, we may gain understanding of what kind of person Phoebe was likely to have been.

How to Use This Book

First, actually write down answers to the study questions! The questions are designed to help you process the information that you're seeing in each chapter. Writing down your answers will help you to explore the evidence fully and articulate your ideas about this complex subject. You may have some interesting insights as you go, and this way you won't forget any of them. By the end, you may want to look back at what you studied in earlier chapters. (You can use a notebook if you don't want to write in your book.)

Second, it can be hard to restrain yourself and not to dive in immediately and start talking about the implications of this study for what women do in your church. I understand that. But try not to reach any firm conclusions until the end, so you can consider all the various aspects of the biblical material. Again, it's a good idea to write down your observations as you go. It's a lot to think about, and for many Christians there are implications for our modern practices. The concluding chapter is designed to help you apply your knowledge of the ancient world to the situation in your own church.

Thoughts for Readers Who Are Using This Book as Part of a Group Study

First, encourage your group members to write down answers to the study questions.

Second, you can help each other to become better readers of Scripture by asking one another to identify wording in the passage that leads you to draw your conclusions. The examples I give also try to do this by citing phrases from the New Testament. Sticking close to the language of the text can help you become aware of how you arrived at your understanding, and it can help discussions move to a deeper level.

Third, be open to disagreement about how to interpret biblical passages. That can be threatening in some contexts, but it's entirely possible for faithful readers to have different opinions. The first readers of the New Testament were quite a diverse group too, and they also disagreed about how to interpret Scripture. If you can become aware of how you reach your different conclusions, you'll learn a lot about each other and also about the text you're interpreting.

PART 1

Wealth and Property

1

Property Ownership

What was Phoebe like? The Roman church that received Paul's letter would have had a lot more clues to go on than we do because they were meeting her in person. Other Romans, even just a few weeks or months later, may not have known who Phoebe was, but they probably made some pretty good guesses based on their knowledge of how things worked in their culture.

This chapter describes the legal and social practices that shaped women's property ownership at the time. While we'll never know whether Phoebe was rich or poor, or who paid for her travel, we can learn what was normal in Phoebe's time, and that can help us understand broadly what kind of person she was—and give us skills to figure out information about other New Testament women.

That women owned property was fairly common in this period of Roman life. In fact, women owned about one-third of all property across the Roman Mediterranean territories. (That's actually about the same proportion of wealth that women own nowadays worldwide.) Women were not equal to men in terms of ownership, but they did own a significant amount. Women's property ownership was not something extraordinary but a regular and expected part of the cultural landscape.

Legal and social norms of the first century supported women's ownership of property. Some of these norms contradict what we are used to hearing about the ancient world. For example, many Christians today have the impression that women were under the legal control of their fathers until they married, at which point they came under the legal authority of their husbands. This misrepresents the legal status of women in the New Testament period.

To understand the cultural differences better, let's imagine the lives of a wealthy family using information from legal records and evidence of actual economic and social patterns. We'll call the mother and father Paula and Marcus. They had four children, but let's say that two died, leaving a daughter, Marcella, and a son named Fabius.

Women owned about one-third of all property. According to Roman law, both Marcella and Fabius were under the legal authority of their father for as long as Marcus lived. Marcus's authority meant that he technically owned his property *and* all of his children's property until he died—even when they were grown-ups, and even when they got married and moved elsewhere. Strange, right?

Marcus lived to be fifty years old. When he died, Marcella was twenty-four and Fabius was twenty-two. At that point, they inherited his property and became legally independent. So now Marcella and Fabius are legally the sole owners of the property they inherited from Marcus.

Both law and custom agreed that fathers should give their property in roughly equal proportions to their children. Spouses could inherit a portion of each other's wealth, but the bulk of it went to the children. So Marcella and Fabius became the primary owners of Marcus's property. (He gave about 20 percent of his wealth to his wife, Paula, and he also made smaller gifts to a business partner and a favorite niece and nephew.)

Here are some important things to notice:

- While it is true that daughters were under the legal authority of their fathers, the same authority applied to their brothers as well.

- Legal independence applied to both sons and daughters.
- Both women and men owned property.

Recall that Paula and Marcus were wealthy. Marcella inherited their large estate with extensive olive orchards and a brick factory. Fabius inherited his father's olive press and another farm with vineyards. Although the custom was for children to inherit equally, there was a bias toward sons. In this case, Fabius also inherited the family's house in Rome, which gave him an edge over his elder sister. Some Romans were even richer than Marcus, but frankly, his kids were very well situated upon his death.

Marcus's wife, Paula, was forty-three when she became a widow. But she also owned considerable wealth that she had inherited from her own father when he died. Now she became a little bit richer because she inherited some of Marcus's estate. Paula's father's farm was smaller than the lands Marcus had owned, but she was her father's only living child and became the sole owner of his property. When she died, she passed on some of that property to her children and the rest to members of her father's extended family.

A Widespread Pattern

Paula and Marcella are examples of Roman women, and we know quite a bit about their legal rights from law books. It's less clear what the status of women was in other places the New Testament mentions, like Judea or cities like Corinth, Thessalonika, and Ephesus. Roman citizens were governed by Roman laws no matter where they lived, but other people Rome ruled were allowed to keep their own customs. So it's harder to say exactly what was happening with women in other parts of the Roman Empire.

However, the evidence we have suggests that women in Greece, Asia Minor, Judea, and Egypt also owned property. Records of the local laws and customs of the time have not all survived, so it's hard to know what legal arrangements shaped the lives of women in the provinces. However, there is evidence that women who lived there undertook the same kinds of actions as Roman women with regard to their property. For example, they donated buildings, honored family members with statues, and owned livestock and slaves. Their ability to do these things suggests they controlled property according to legal patterns similar to those of Roman law.

Many women property owners were nowhere near as wealthy as Paula or Marcella. Poorer women were less likely to be able to afford burial inscriptions for their loved ones, and they didn't donate whole buildings, as wealthy women did, leaving a physical record of their actions. Their daily transactions weren't often recorded. Yet, though we have little evidence to inform us of their situation, some records display the property ownership of women of average means. For example, here is a divorce agreement from Egypt (where some paper records have survived, thanks to the dry climate): "Zois acknowledges that she has received from Antipatros by hand from his house clothes to the value of one hundred and twenty drachmas and a pair of gold earrings, which he received as a dowry."[1] This document was a receipt showing that her husband, Antipatros, returned Zois's property after their divorce. Zois and Antipatros were not wealthy people. Nevertheless, Zois owned something.

The evidence we have for Jewish women likewise suggests that they owned property. Many modern readers of the New Testament are conditioned to assume that Jewish women of this period did not share any of the advantages of Greek women. But this is also untrue. Historical sources attest to similar legal and social conventions for Jewish women.

For example, you may know the story of Judith from the apocryphal books of the Bible. (The Apocrypha consists of books written in Greek between the time of the Old and New Testaments. Some Christians—Roman Catholics, for example—consider them part of the Bible today. But even if they're not part of your Bible, they are still helpful documents because they give us more historical information about the same time period.) Here's some of the information we get about Judith: "Her husband Manasseh had left her gold and silver, men and women slaves, livestock, and fields; and she maintained this estate. No one spoke ill of her, for she feared God with great devotion" (Jth. 8:7–8).[2] This story conveys the social expectation that women could be property owners. Readers were unlikely to be surprised that Judith had wealth. Her story is told in a way that suggests this was a familiar pattern.

Women owned the same kinds of property that men did.

Historical sources confirm that some Jewish women were incredibly wealthy, while others like Zois owned only a little, and many others were in between. But in all these areas, ownership wasn't limited to elite women or to those who were Roman citizens. Women all across the Mediterranean had some property to call their own.

Women owned the same kinds of property that men did as well. They owned farmland and animals, houses and apartment buildings, businesses and equipment. Women also possessed clothing, jewelry, and household goods, items that weren't disposable, as they often are today, but were handed down to one's children. Many people owned slaves, and documents from the period record both men and women buying and selling enslaved people.

New Testament Women

These same patterns of property ownership are visible in the New Testament. Women owned property in varying amounts. Some, like the widow with the two coins, had very little, while others were *very* wealthy, like Bernice, the daughter of Herod Agrippa, who appears at the end of Acts. Most women were probably somewhere in between. Their property ownership doesn't often come directly into view in the New Testament because it's not really the subject of these writings. But ancient readers, who were familiar with these patterns, would have assumed that most of the women they saw in these passages owned some property.

Let's use the example of the widow with two coins to think about how this historical evidence is useful as we read the New Testament. Afterward, you can apply the same principles to other passages. Here's the way Mark tells her story:

> Jesus sat down opposite the place where the offerings were put and watched the crowd putting their money into the temple treasury. Many rich people threw in large amounts. But a poor widow came and put in two very small copper coins, worth only a few pence. Calling to his disciples, Jesus said, "Truly, I tell you, this poor widow has put more into the treasury than all the others. They all gave out of their wealth; but she, out of her poverty, put in everything—all she had to live on." (Mark 12:41–44)

If we have the expectation that women can own property, we may see that reflected in this story. However, rather than assume that it's true, we need to look for clues in the wording of the story that would have supported this idea for early readers of Mark's Gospel. Here's a basic set of steps to follow when interpreting a passage like this.

First, look in the passage to identify wording that suggests the woman is a property owner. In this case, she has "two very small copper coins" (v. 42). That Jesus says they are "all she had" (v. 44) underscores that she is the owner. Also, the story wouldn't make any sense if the coins didn't belong to her. Why would it be noble to give away someone else's money? Thus, it seems right to say the money belongs to her.

Second, identify the wording in the passage that suggests whether she is poor, wealthy, or in between. In this case, it's easy, because she is twice identified as "poor" (vv. 42, 43). She is also contrasted with "many rich people" (v. 41) who have a lot of money to donate. However, we also see that the two copper coins are "worth only a few pence" (v. 42), and that is "all she had" (v. 44). It seems fair to conclude that she is a very poor person.

What about the detail that tells us she is a "widow" (v. 42)? Many readers assume that all widows were left without resources. But we remember from the examples of Paula and Judith earlier in this chapter that widows weren't always poor. So, knowing that she's a widow doesn't actually give us information about her wealth.

Third, consider what we don't know about this woman. You may have a lot of questions about her: Was she recently widowed? How did she continue to live if she gave away all her money? Did she have other family members still living? These are interesting questions, but the passage doesn't give us any clues to answer them. It's important to acknowledge both what the passage can tell us and what it doesn't tell us about this woman and her social status.

With the passages below, you can do the same thing, applying what you know from the chapter to think about the meaning of New Testament passages in a way that assumes that women owned property.

PARABLE OF A WOMAN WHO LOSES A COIN

"Or suppose a woman has ten silver coins and loses one. Doesn't she light a lamp, sweep the house and search carefully until she finds it? And when she finds it, she calls her friends and neighbors together and says, 'Rejoice with me; I have found my lost coin.' In the same way, I tell you, there is rejoicing in the presence of the angels of God over one sinner who repents." (Luke 15:8–10)

1. Look in the passage to identify wording that would suggest to ancient readers that the woman is a property owner.

2. Identify the wording in the passage that would suggest whether she is poor, wealthy, or in between.

3. Identify the questions you have about the woman or details the story does not provide.

WOMAN ANOINTING JESUS

While he was at Bethany, reclining at the table in the home of Simon the Leper, a woman came with an alabaster jar of very expensive perfume, made of pure nard. She broke the jar and poured the perfume on his head. Some of those present were saying indignantly to one another, "Why this waste of perfume? It could have been sold for more than a year's wages and the money given to the poor." And they rebuked her harshly. (Mark 14:3–5)

1. Identify wording in the passage that would suggest to ancient readers that the woman is a property owner.

2. Identify wording in the passage that would suggest whether she is poor, wealthy, or in between.

3. Identify the questions you have about the woman or details the story does not provide.

WOMAN WITH A HEMORRHAGE

And a woman was there who had been subject to bleeding for twelve years. She had suffered a great deal under the care of many doctors and had spent all she had, yet instead of getting better she grew worse. When she heard about Jesus, she came up behind him in the crowd and touched his cloak, because she thought, "If I just touch his clothes, I will be healed." Immediately her bleeding stopped and she felt in her body that she was freed from her suffering. (Mark 5:25–29)

1. Identify wording in the passage that would suggest to ancient readers that the woman is a property owner.

2. Identify wording in the passage that would suggest whether she is poor, wealthy, or in between.

3. Identify the questions you have about the woman or details the story does not provide.

4. Use the space below to write your reflections about women's property in the New Testament. You might also note other passages that you want to look up or any new ideas you have as a result of this chapter.

2

Property Management

L ike other women of her day, Phoebe was a property owner. As we saw in the previous chapter, women didn't possess as much property as men, but they owned enough that women's ownership was a normal part of everyday life. We can't yet say anything about how wealthy Phoebe was or what she did with her property. Some women owned only a little property and some owned a lot; it depended on their social status.

But you might be wondering whether Phoebe was really the one in control of her property. Did she decide what to do with it? Were men actually the real property managers and women only the owners on paper? This chapter explores the evidence that addresses these questions—though the short answer is that women owned their own property and made decisions about what to do with it.

Women Honored for Using Their Wealth

One kind of evidence for women managing their property is the inscriptions like the one to Junia Rustica that we read in the first chapter. Her city honored Junia for her many gifts to the place in which she lived. And the wording described Junia as the one doing all these things. At the end of the introductory chapter, you listed verbs that conveyed Junia's actions, words and phrases like "gave," "reimbursed," "set up," "gave at her own cost," "made and dedicated at her own cost." The inscription attributes all of this activity to Junia, and it explicitly notes that she did this with her own money. Junia's husband is mentioned, but not as the one in charge. The text portrays Junia as the one whose actions led to these benefits.

Many wealthy women were honored in inscriptions like the one to Junia Rustica, particularly for their public benefactions. Here is another one: "Ummidia Quadratilla, daughter of Gaius, built the amphitheater and the temple for the citizens of Casina from her own resources."[1] This is an example of an elite woman from Italy. We get a sense of the scope of her resources from the fact that she built both an amphitheater and a temple, both enormous and costly buildings.

But Ummidia's wealth was actually even more extensive than this, and her name was attested in other inscriptions in the same town. She restored the decaying theater that her father had originally gifted the town, in so doing both restoring honor to her family in general (since it was already her father's gift) and increasing her own status. In addition, Ummidia paid for a banquet for the town to celebrate the theater's renovation. In *Women owned their own property and made decisions about what to do with it.* short, like Junia Rustica, Ummidia was one of the wealthiest people in her town. Her gifts helped to sustain the kind of civic events that had become popular in the New Testament period.

Literary records also amplify our picture of Ummidia. A high-ranking government official named Pliny the Younger, writing shortly after her death, spoke of her as the "leading woman" of her city.[2] That wording was often used to indicate the status of wealthy individuals within their city of origin. Both women and men were identified as "leading" or "first" among the citizens in their town.

Leaders like Ummidia undertook substantial roles as patrons of their communities. Acts of patronage weren't something wealthy people had to do, so the community often expressed its thanks in an inscription. Ummidia's inscription notes her agency by giving her credit for undertaking these actions.

Most women were not wealthy. But they often owned some property, and they took action to use, sustain, and grow their property. One kind of evidence for such actions is tax records of property registrations. An example from Egypt records a woman named Taouetis owning six camels: "The six camels in the vicinity of the village which

Both women and men were identified as "leading" or "first" among the citizens in their town.

I registered in the previous 20th year I also now register for the present 21st year of the lord Hadrian Caesar, at Soknopaiou Nesos."[3] Soknopaiou Nesos was a village at the edge of the desert in Egypt. Having and using camels to haul goods across deserts was an important part of its economy. This document is Taouetis's receipt showing her payment of taxes for and registration of her six camels. There are also similar records of men's ownership of camels, and they all share a similar format and wording. The records show women like Taouetis participating in their local economy in ways that were conventional in their villages.

Other examples of women's actions with their property include the purchase of burial plots. For example, Rufina, a Jewish woman in Asia Minor, left this marker for a burial place she erected: "Rufina, a Jew, head of the synagogue, built this tomb for her freed slaves and the slaves raised in her house."[4] Rufina was the owner of a household, enslaved people, and this burial place. She also held the title *archisynogōgos*, which means "leader of the synagogue." Rufina was not a Roman citizen or one of the wealthiest people in her city, but she had some property and social standing. The inscription makes it clear that she's the one responsible for establishing the burial place.

There seem to have been social mechanisms to enforce the intentions expressed in Rufina's inscription, for the next portion of the text reads, "No one else has the right to bury anyone here. Anyone who dares to do so will pay 1500 *denaria* to the sacred treasury and 1000 *denaria* to the Jewish people. A copy of this inscription has been placed in the public archives." Rufina's words convey the expectation that her wishes regarding her property will be respected. She participates in the same socially agreed-upon practices that others did when they established burial places.

Evidence like this gives us a glimpse into the lives of real women in the New Testament period. The wealthiest people sponsored grand building projects and community events. Less wealthy women took part in their local economies and in cultural practices like burial. They put their property to use, following the same conventions and patterns that men did. Though overall men owned more property than women, women still owned a substantial amount, and they used their property in many of the same ways men did.

Household Management

Managing property and managing household affairs were in fact women's jobs. According to traditional gender expectations of the time, "women's work" was not only cooking and cleaning but also many of the tasks that kept the household going. Married women often were responsible for supervising their husband's property as well as their own. Even though Roman law insisted that the ownership of property by the husband and wife had to be kept separate, the wife conducted many of the day-to-day affairs of the whole household.

We see this pattern of responsibilities in the writing of an ancient author named Columella, who lists the responsibilities of the woman in charge of a farm.[5] Though she was not the owner of the farm, her duties included inspecting the quality of everything that came into the house and maintaining and organizing stores of food and supplies, including grain, wine, utensils, furniture, clothing, and weapons. She was also

Married women often were responsible for supervising their husband's property.

in charge of supervising the time-consuming production of clothing for everyone in the household, and she oversaw the cooking and the upkeep of the barns and animals—no small job!

Papyrus records of Egypt confirm that women did many of the things Columella wrote about. Here's a letter from an Egyptian woman named Diogenis to her property manager, Kronion: "Sell the wheat and collect the bronze at your house while I come, because I need it. Go to Myrtale and ask her for the money. If she does not want to give it to you, lock her up. See that I do not come and find the wall built up. And . . . let the dining room be paved, according to the arrangement Aphys wants; shake out the woolen cloths and the clothes and watch the children and things at home. Watch little Isadora. I pray that you are well."[6]

Diogenis seems to feel pretty comfortable giving instructions to Kronion. Even if we can't tell exactly what she means—like why she doesn't want to find the wall built up—she clearly intends her wishes to be carried out. She is giving instructions about agricultural products, collecting money that is owed to her, specifying renovations to a house, and directing the care of children, clothing, and other household fabrics.

Diogenis's letter doesn't specify who owns the property that she mentions: the wheat, bronze, money, dining room, woolen cloths, and clothing. If Diogenis is married, it is likely that some of the items in the instructions legally belonged to her husband. But some may also have been her own property. There's no way to know. It's also possible that Diogenis was a widow, and that all this property now belonged to her. No matter the circumstances, it's clear that Diogenis exercises considerable authority in managing the affairs of her household.

Diogenis wasn't doing anything unusual in sending this letter with instructions to her property manager. In fact, Columella's own list suggests that the instructions Diogenis gives here were the kinds of actions that were routinely expected of women and were considered to be virtuous. (We'll talk more about these expectations in chapter 9 when we talk about industry as a virtue.)

New Testament Property Management

Women in the New Testament also owned property. And, similar to other women of the time, they made decisions about how to manage their wealth. Married women oversaw their house- holds, and thus managed part of their husband's   *Managing the household* wealth as well. And managing the household was a   *was a complex task!* complex task! Rather than simply cooking a quick meal, for example, feeding a family involved the whole process of procuring food or growing one's own. Women often saw to family business interests as well as other household needs.

Consider the evidence in the New Testament stories below for women's agency with respect to their property. We can continue to identify the fact of women's property ownership, as we did in the previous chapter. And we can consider how ancient readers would have understood these women's authority over their property.

THE WOMAN WHO ANOINTS JESUS

All four Gospels tell the story of a woman who anoints Jesus, though the details of each vary quite a bit. In the last chapter, we looked at Mark's version, but now let's consider Matthew's:

> While Jesus was in Bethany at the home of Simon the Leper, a woman came to him with an alabaster jar of very expensive per- fume, which she poured on his head as he was reclining at the ta- ble. When the disciples saw this, they were indignant. "Why this waste?" they asked. "This perfume could have been sold at a high price and the money given to the poor." Aware of this, Jesus said to them, "Why are you bothering this woman? She has done a beautiful thing to me. The poor you will always have with you, but you will not always have me. When she poured this perfume on my body, she did it to prepare me for burial. Truly I tell you, wherever

this gospel is preached throughout the world, what she has done will also be told, in memory of her." (Matt. 26:6–13)

1. Look in the passage to identify wording that would suggest to ancient readers that this woman is a property owner.

2. Identify the wording in the passage that suggests that she managed or controlled her own property.

3. Identify the questions you have about the woman or details the story does not provide.

LYDIA

One of those listening was a woman from the city of Thyatira named Lydia, a dealer in purple cloth. She was a worshiper of God. The Lord opened her heart to respond to Paul's message. When she and the members of her household were baptized, she invited us to her home. "If you consider me a believer in the Lord," she said, "come and stay at my house." And she persuaded us. (Acts 16:14–15)

1. Look in the passage to identify wording that would suggest to ancient readers that Lydia is a property owner.

2. Identify the wording in the passage that suggests that Lydia managed her property.

3. Identify the questions you have about the woman or details the story does not provide.

REFLECTIONS

Use the space below to write your reflections about women's property management in the New Testament. You might note other passages that come to mind that you want to look up, or you might write down any new ideas you have as a result of this chapter.

Marriage

Was Phoebe married? We don't know. Paul doesn't mention a husband, but perhaps only because he was not involved in the Jesus movement. (By contrast, in the next verses, Paul greets a married couple, Prisca and Aquila.)

Many interpreters argue that social norms around marriage restricted women's freedom. They regard unmarried or widowed women as people with greater capacity for independent action. On that basis, some interpret Phoebe as one of these women whose unmarried status allowed her to take on leadership roles in the church.

In this chapter, we'll consider how marriage or divorce affected the legal and social status of women. It turns out that most married women were not under the legal authority of their husbands. Husbands usually had more social standing than their wives, and therefore more power. But cultural norms gave women more power than we might expect.

The Legal Status of Married Women

In chapter 1, we saw how Roman women gained legal independence when their fathers died. In this period, a father had legal authority over his sons and daughters, and he was technically the owner of their wealth until he died. At that point, children inherited from their father, and that property legally belonged to them.

Let's remember our imaginary Roman family from chapter 1. Both Marcella and her brother Fabius were under the legal authority of their father, Marcus. When he died, they became legally independent and inherited property from him. That meant they became owners with rights over their own property.

Marcella was twenty-four when her father died, and she was already married. What effect did that have on her property rights? None. Whether or not the daughter was married, she became the owner of her property once her father died. The event that changed a person's legal status wasn't marriage: it was the death of the father. When he died, both son and daughter became legally independent.

This independent status meant that most wives were *never* under the legal authority of their husbands. This point is quite different from what most modern people expect. We've been taught that women couldn't own property. We've been taught that anything to which a woman had a right would be controlled by her husband, because he exercised all legal authority. That was true for Romans a couple of centuries earlier, but no longer in New Testament times.

Most married women were not under the legal authority of their husbands.

A father had legal authority over other members of his household, but *not* over his wife. She remained under the authority of her father if he was alive, and if he had died, she was legally independent. Her husband would likewise be under the legal authority of his father, if his father was still living. For both men and women, legal independence was not affected by marital status. If a woman was legally independent, her husband did not control her property.

Property Ownership in Marriage

Romans viewed the property of husband and wife as legally separate. This point was quite important, and a number of laws reinforced it. For example, it was actually illegal for spouses to give gifts to one another! The idea was that if you gave your spouse a gift, you were giving your birth family's wealth away to your spouse's family. Over time, Roman law changed to accommodate the practice of spouses giving gifts to each other. But the idea behind the law was important: families of both the husband and the wife should retain the rights to their own properties.

Let's consider Marcella and Fabius's mother, Paula. She was married to Marcus, who died when he was fifty and she was forty-five. Although Marcus had legal authority over their children and owned all of the children's property until he died, Paula owned property throughout their marriage. Being married didn't mean that Paula's property belonged to Marcus. The couple saw their interests as joined together, and so they talked about what they might do with their combined wealth. But each one viewed the other as the owner of that person's respective property.

An interesting feature of their financial lives was Paula's dowry. When Paula married Marcus, her father arranged for a portion of the lands that Paula would inherit to be given to Marcus as her dowry. The dowry was property that came under the control of the husband during the marriage, and he could benefit from the use of it during the marriage. However, both the law and society viewed the dowry as belonging to the wife. That meant that Marcus could farm the land and sell the produce and benefit from that money, but he couldn't sell the land and spend the money. It wasn't really his to sell. And, most importantly, when Marcus died (or if the couple divorced), the land became Paula's property again.

Law and society viewed the dowry as belonging to the wife.

Dowries in this period represented a portion of a woman's wealth, not all of it. So Paula continued to own much of the land adjacent to the plot that became her dowry. The dowry illustrates the relative power imbalance of husbands over wives, for it placed property in the husband's control in a way that had no parallel for women. Nevertheless, women of the period owned property that was not included in their dowries.

Dowries varied in size according to a woman's social status, but they were not extravagant compared to those in some other cultures and periods in history. Paula's dowry was a relatively large plot of land, bigger than the sum total of some families' wealth. But it wasn't that large relative to the wealth that she and Marcus owned overall. Here's an example of a much smaller dowry from a woman named Thatres who lived in Egypt: "The dowry given is sixty silver drachmas and . . . a pair of gold earrings of three quarters (weight) and a gold crescent necklace of one and a half (quarters weight) and silver armlets of eight drachmas of uncoined bullion (weight) and a bronze basin and two bronze water-jars and tin utensils of two minas weight."[1] Although it's impossible to tell the total wealth of the couple involved, this dowry is small relative to other records of the time. But the wife would have owned other possessions that were not included in the dowry.

Actually, Thatres's marriage document is an example of one type of contract from that time in Egypt, in which the husband also specified what property he ceded to his wife during the marriage. In this case, the husband had inherited from his mother a portion of a house and courtyard, and he gave that to Thatres, along with some of the other possessions that he might acquire during their marriage. Now, Roman citizens would never have had a contract like that. So we see that practices varied across the Roman Empire. But in each case we also see women owning property in substantial amounts.

Jewish women also owned property during their marriages. One small archive of documents from the second century records financial transactions of a Jewish woman named Babatha. One of the documents records a loan she made of three hundred silver denarii to her second husband, Judah. The legal record is similar to those of loans that were made outside of the family. The husband stated he would "return them to her at any time that she will wish."[2] Another document registered Babatha's land, which was used to farm dates and barley.

Understanding the Evidence

Interpreting this evidence can be difficult because of two misconceptions we often hold about ancient women. The first is the assumption that marriage limited women's abilities to play such roles. We have been told that women were controlled by their husbands during marriage and were unable to exercise significant leadership. Along with the legal norms I described in chapter 1, the inscriptions suggest that this was not the case. Both married and unmarried women served in these roles.

In the Greek cities of the eastern part of the empire where Paul traveled, many women held civic and administrative titles that identified their roles as patrons. Here is an example from Chios, an island near Ephesus: "For Claudia Metrodora, daughter of Skytheinos, gymnasiarch four times, who twice distributed oil to the city on the occasion of the festival of the Heraklea games;

Women's officeholding   *agōnothetē* three times of the Heraklea Romaia and
was not determined by   Kaisareia; queen of the thirteen cities of the Ionian
their marital status.   federation, being desirous of glory for the city . . . a
lover of her homeland and priestess for life of the divine empress Aphrodite Livia, by reason of her excellence and admirable behavior towards it."[3]

Through this inscription, the city honored Claudia for her concrete acts of civic benefaction. These acts included the distribution of food to citizens of Chios, the organization of games at an important religious festival, and a priesthood. That Claudia is called "queen . . . of the Ionian federation" here suggests her political leadership in coordinating action among local cities.

Other inscriptions identify Claudia as a city magistrate (*stephanē-phoros*) on two separate occasions. What is unusual about the inscriptions honoring Claudia is not the fact that a woman held office but the quantity of titles she held. Although women appeared less frequently than men in these honorary inscriptions, they often had the same titles as did men in similar positions.

Inscriptions found in Ephesus identify the same person, Claudia Metrodora, as a married woman. She contributed with her husband to civic benefactions in that city. But Claudia's titles were different from the titles her husband held, and he was not mentioned at all in the inscriptions from Chios that honored her. Other evidence from the area around Ephesus shows that some women who held civic office were married while others were unmarried. These patterns in the inscriptions have led scholars to conclude that women's officeholding was not determined by their marital status.

Divorce

Cultures of this period valued long marriages and praised individuals who were devoted to one spouse throughout their lives. However, divorce was also readily available and could be seen as the right option to pursue under certain circumstances. In fact, Emperor Augustus passed legislation that required a Roman man to divorce his wife if she committed adultery.

Divorce could be initiated by either the husband or the wife. It wasn't necessary to get permission from a judge to obtain a divorce. If two people stopped considering themselves married, then the law considered them divorced.

People today often assume that ancient women would not have left their husbands, especially because (they assume) they had no financial resources of their own. But now we know that wasn't true: women did own property, and their husbands had to return their dowries if the couple divorced. Under those circumstances, it seems reasonable that some women would have found divorce to be a good option.

Since divorce required no documentation, it's really difficult to tell how common divorce was or how often individuals divorced. Ancient historians and letter writers sometimes mention elite couples who divorced and married someone else in order to forge new political alli-

ances between their families. Other times divorce becomes apparent
when parties sought a court document to verify the return of the dowry.

A Jewish woman could   Although legal intervention wasn't required for the
also initiate a divorce.   divorce itself, the courts could offer a kind of receipt
                            so that the husband couldn't be sued down the road by
                            someone (either his former wife or her next husband,
say) claiming he hadn't repaid the dowry.

In chapter 1, I mentioned Zois's legal document returning her
dowry to her as evidence of a woman owning property. In that case,
Zois and her husband, Antipatros, both agreed "that they have sepa-
rated from one another, severing the union which they had formed"
only five months prior.[4] Zois also acknowledged receipt of her dowry
and promised no further legal action would be taken against Antipatros regarding its return.

In another such document, a woman, Tryphaine, petitioned the
court for the return of her dowry. She asserted that her husband
"squandered [the dowry], abused and insulted [her]."[5] In cases like
this when the divorce was not amicable, the woman could petition
the court for the return of her property.

A Jewish woman could also initiate a divorce from her husband.
Some Jewish writings suggest that only men could give their wives
a certificate of divorce. However, other sources suggest that women
obtained divorces as well. The Jewish philosopher Philo, for example,
wrote that women divorced their husbands "for any cause," though
he lamented the practice.[6]

Marriage and Women's Actions in the New Testament

It's often hard to tell the marital status of women in the New Testament.
Was the hemorrhaging woman who touched Jesus's cloak a married
person? How about the woman who begged Jesus to heal her daughter?
Many passages say nothing about whether the characters were married,
widowed, or divorced because it's not important for the story.

Moreover, there wasn't a separate vocabulary word for "wife." The Greek word *gynē* meant both "woman" and "wife." Occasionally the context helps us specify which is meant—for example, when Matthew says that Joseph "did what the angel of the Lord had commanded him and took Mary home as his wife" (1:24). But it's often not possible to tell if *gynē* indicates a married woman.

Likewise, if there wasn't a reason to mention a woman's spouse, then writers would often leave him out. For example, John's Gospel indicates that four women stood near Jesus's cross: his mother, his mother's sister, Mary the wife of Clopas, and Mary Magdalene. Only one woman's husband is mentioned in this group. It seems likely in this case that the author mentioned the husband in order to distinguish her from the other women named Mary.

Similarly, a woman's property ownership isn't what the gospel authors were usually interested in. They were focused on telling the story of Jesus, not the financial state of his followers. As a result, we don't find out much (or anything) about how much property women owned. What did any of these Marys do for a living? Were they rich or poor? How much property did they own? For the most part, there is no way to answer these questions.

The New Testament offers only a few instances in which women who are explicitly stated to be married are mentioned in relationship to their property. One is when Luke mentions women who support the Jesus movement out of their own resources (Luke 8:1–3). One of them is "Joanna the wife of Chuza, manager of Herod's household." Joanna was a married woman who had wealth at her disposal and became a patron of Jesus and his followers. (We'll talk more about patrons in part 2.) Her husband is likely mentioned here because of his social status. Although not elite, his proximity to power gave him social standing. Even though Joanna is married, she is still mentioned here managing her resources in this way.

Since the New Testament authors often don't tell us a character's marital status, let's revisit three stories from the previous chapters.

We have tended to see marriage as something that placed restrictions on women. Based on what you've learned in this chapter, reconsider whether being married would make a difference for the characters' actions in these stories.

THE PARABLE OF THE WOMAN WITH TEN COINS

"Or suppose a woman (*gynē*) has ten silver coins and she loses one. Doesn't she light a lamp, sweep the house and search carefully until she finds it? And when she finds it, she calls her friends and neighbors together and says 'Rejoice with me; I have found my lost coin.' In the same way, I tell you, there is rejoicing in the presence of the angels of God over one sinner who repents." (Luke 15:8–10)

1. List the actions of the woman in the parable.

2. State whether married women did these things.

3. Identify the questions you have about the woman or details the story does not provide.

WOMAN ANOINTING JESUS

While [Jesus] was at Bethany, reclining at the table in the home of Simon the Leper, a woman (*gynē*) came with an alabaster jar of very expensive perfume, made of pure nard. She broke the jar and poured the perfume on his head. Some of those present were saying indignantly to one another, "Why this waste of perfume? It could have been sold for more than a year's wages and the money given to the poor." And they rebuked her harshly. (Mark 14:3–5)

1. List the actions of the woman in the story.

2. State whether married women did these things.

3. Identify the questions you have about the woman or details the story does not provide.

RECONSIDERING PHOEBE

We began this chapter with the question of whether Phoebe was married or unmarried. So let's reconsider the verses about Phoebe based on what you know now.

> I commend to you our sister Phoebe, a deacon of the church in Cenchreae. I ask you to receive her in the Lord in a way worthy of his people and to give her any help she may need from you, for she has been the benefactor of many people, including me. (Rom. 16:1–2)

1. List any details about Phoebe that you want to consider.

2. State whether married women did these things.

3. Identify the questions you have about the woman or details the story does not provide.

4

Occupations

W hat did Phoebe do for a living? Paul calls her "a benefactor of many people," which tells us she had money. But where did her wealth come from? Though we don't know specifically what Phoebe did for a living, there is more we can learn about the work of women in general in this period.

It's safe to say that most women worked hard. Keeping any household running in those days before the Industrial Revolution required considerable labor. The many steps of production involved merely in putting food on the table and clothing on everyone's back meant that all able members of the household had work to do. Few could afford much leisure.

During the New Testament period, there were some changes in the kinds of work people did. In the cities, cloth was available for purchase by this time, so each family didn't have to create its own. There were also restaurants at which poorer people ate. But this didn't mean people had less work to do. For most people, it just meant that instead of carding wool, growing crops, and collecting wood and water, their days were filled with other tasks. Women and men both worked hard to keep their families going.

Women had a variety of jobs—and more than you might think!

Women had a variety of jobs—and more than you might think! We know about some of their activities from burial inscriptions that state the deceased person's occupation. These inscriptions were meant to honor the dead, so the fact that their occupation was listed suggests that it was a point of pride. Men are recorded as participating in a wider variety of jobs than women, but women nonetheless did many different kinds of work.

Motherhood and Child Rearing

One kind of labor we typically associate with women is raising children. Men were also viewed as responsible for children's upbringing and were sometimes employed to care for children. But most of the laborers were probably women.

And there were plenty of babies that needed care! The population size was stable during the New Testament period, but child mortality was high: about half of all children died before age five, and of course, people died for various reasons after that point without reaching old age. So, if the total number of people was stable, scholars estimate that each woman had five or six pregnancies on average.

Some women worked in paid employment as wet nurses. Families employed a wet nurse to care for a young child for various reasons. Wealthier families often did so to allow the mother time to do other things besides nursing. Families also needed a wet nurse if the mother had died in childbirth (there was of course no infant formula in those days!). And some sought a wet nurse for an enslaved infant whose mother was not part of the family. A number of contracts for wet nurses still exist, showing evidence of this practice and the terms of employment.

Interestingly, wealthier families also regarded the choice of a wet nurse as an important part of their child's early education. Some writers indicate that it was important that she speak Greek, for example, so the child would learn the language from a native speaker, starting at a young age. Others mention that she should be of strong character. So clearly wet nurses were doing more than just feeding children; they were teaching and nurturing as well.

Some women were elementary and secondary teachers. There are only a few references to this, but none of them suggests surprise at women being teachers. One letter by a woman to her husband, who is away in the military, assures him, "Do not worry about the children. They are well and attend [the lessons of] a woman teacher."[1] One burial portrait of a woman named Hermione identifies her as a teacher of grammar and literature.

Household Management

Women directed a lot of their labor toward management of the household. As we saw in chapter 2, managing the household was considered women's work. Although the job description varied significantly depending on whether they managed a large villa in Rome or a small country farm, this was labor in which many women were actively engaged.

But household labor involved a different set of tasks compared to today. Nowadays, women who tend to their home and children are often thought of as either "not working" or as "not working outside the home." They don't go out to a job like others do. They're not employed. It's easy to let this color our view of ancient women and their job of household management. But we want to try to learn how ancient people viewed women's work—because things were different then.

When ancient people thought of a household—or of the "private" arena—they thought not only of feeding and clothing household members, but also of all the business and social endeavors of the family. Business was considered part of "private" life. So even though ancient people imagined "women's work" as focusing on the household, it involved a whole lot more than what we consider household chores today.

Back in chapter 2, I mentioned a woman named Diogenis who wrote a letter giving instructions about family business matters. She told a male worker to sell the wheat, collect bronze items, collect money from someone who owed it, shake out woolen cloth, and look after the children. Today we would consider the last two of these parts of household management. But for ancient people, the first three items were, too. Women's household work included business affairs.

Here's another example from Egypt. A woman named Thais writes to Tigrios, someone she employs to help manage her business interests: "If you come, take out six measures of vegetable seed and seal them in sacks so that they are ready, and if you can, go up and look for the donkey. Sarapodora and Sabinos greet you. Do not sell the young pigs without me. Farewell."[2] Again, this woman sends instructions about how to handle matters regarding her family's livelihood. When she was at home, Thais would simply have said these things to Tigrios, which, of course, we don't have a record of. So these letters give us insight into the kinds of tasks women considered their responsibility.

Wealthier women had more people to help them in their work, but they also had more (and larger) business dealings to manage. In Pompeii, the Roman city that was preserved when Vesuvius erupted and covered it in ash, some signs were preserved, including this one: "On the estate of Julia Felix, the daughter of Spurius Felix, the following are for rent: an elegant bath suitable for the best people, shops, rooms above them, and second story apartments."[3] Julia had a lot of property, and we see one aspect of her household dealings in this rental notice.

Women's household work included business affairs.

Some women who owned land went into the business of making bricks. There were lots of grand buildings erected in this period, and bricks were big business. The brickmakers often stamped their bricks with a seal, which included the name of the owner and the production manager. Some of the owners were women, and some managers were as well. So in this example, owning land became an opportunity for the woman to develop a business, using her land as a resource.

Wealthier households exploited the labor of enslaved people to accomplish their work. The women who ran those households were often slave owners themselves, along with their husbands. For these women, part of their job was managing the labor of the enslaved members of the household.

Some of the jobs of enslaved women are known because of their funeral inscriptions stating their name and occupation. Many were personal servants of the free women of the household. Hairdressers played an important role because of the elaborate hairstyles that were fashionable. Wearing such a hairstyle was itself a mark of status because of the amount of leisure time required to create and maintain it, and the fact that they could own a slave whose time was dedicated to this purpose. Other jobs noted in inscriptions include *vestiplicae* (those who cared for clothing) and *pedisequae* (those who ran errands for the matron or accompanied her when she went out). It was more common for enslaved men to have the clerical jobs within the home, but women occasionally did these jobs too.

Other Occupations

Some women's jobs were things we associate with traditional women's work, only on a larger scale. For example, as the production of cloth moved from homes to factories, women had jobs as spinners and textile workers. Some women worked independently of the factories, making contracts with local families to provide thread or yarn, or to make or mend clothing.

But women worked in a wide variety of occupations that extended beyond normal household chores. They were mosaic workers and jewelers, musicians, singers, and actors. Many *Women worked in a wide* women sold produce, meat, and other prod- *variety of occupations.* ucts in the markets. Some women owned and ran restaurants.

Some occupations of women seem surprising to us today. For example, while we may expect women to be midwives, they were also doctors and healers. One burial inscription reads: "To Primilla, a physician, daughter of Lucius Vibius Melito. She lived 44 years, 30 of which she spent with Lucius Coecceius Apthorus without a quarrel. Apthorus built this monument for his best, chaste wife and for himself."[4] A number of other inscriptions simply recorded the woman's name with her occupation: "doctor."

A few inscriptions and literary references commemorate women gladiators and athletes. The picture in figure 1 shows two women gladiators fighting. The inscription commemorates their freedom: "Amazon and Achillia were granted a reprieve."[5]

Figure 1. Marble relief featuring female gladiators; the British Museum

These occupations are often known to us now because someone thought the profession was honorable and took the time to commemorate it in stone. Many women's epigraphs mentioned their profession, though it was by no means required to do so. The fact that people chose to remember women in this way suggests that their work was a source of pride. Other sources likewise honored women's excellence in their professions. For example, one inscription from the city of

Delphi in Greece honored a woman harp player for her excellent performance. Taken as a whole, such inscriptions reinforce the idea that society approved of women working in a variety of occupations.

These sources only give us hints about what women's working lives were like. But they certainly convey that women worked in a variety of professions, that they took pride in their work, and that other people appreciated and applauded their excellence. None of the sources find fault with the women for working outside of the home or suggest in any way that their work was unconventional. Indeed, the city and household depended on the labor of women to achieve the level of economic prosperity that was common in this period.

Occupations of Women in the New Testament

Most of the time, the stories of the New Testament don't give any indication of the work women did or the occupations they held. Some passages reinforce the impression that we have of women's domestic labor. For example, Martha served Jesus at a dinner party (Luke 10:38–42; John 12:1–8), and Peter's mother-in-law served Jesus after he healed her (Mark 1:29–31). These stories occur within a household setting and place women in domestic roles.

But the work that women did outside the household was also culturally important, and the first readers of the New Testament probably assumed that all these women worked in some capacity. What did the Samaritan woman do for a living (John 4:7–26), or the Canaanite woman (Matt. 15:21–28)? For that matter, what kind of work did Mary, Jesus's mother, do? Or her cousin Elizabeth? None of these women's occupations are mentioned. But the social reality suggests that all of them worked hard for the sake of their families and communities.

Only a few passages explicitly point to the labor of women. Read the following passages and consider the ways that women and their work are visible in the New Testament.

PAUL ENCOUNTERS LYDIA

Luke mentions a few details about Lydia in her encounter with Paul in Acts 16.

> On the Sabbath we went outside the city gate to the river, where we expected to find a place of prayer. We sat down and began to speak to the women who had gathered there. One of those listening was a woman from the city of Thyatira named Lydia, a dealer in purple cloth. She was a worshiper of God. The Lord opened her heart to respond to Paul's message. When she and the members of her household were baptized, she invited us to her home. "If you consider me a believer in the Lord," she said, "come and stay at my house." And she persuaded us. (Acts 16:13–15)

1. What kind of work was this woman doing?

2. With whom did she work?

3. What details about the story interest you, and what do you wish you knew more about?

PRISCILLA

Acts also gives us a snippet of information about Priscilla.

> After this, Paul left Athens and went to Corinth. There he met a Jew named Aquila, a native of Pontus, who had recently come from Italy with his wife Priscilla, because Claudius had ordered all Jews

to leave Rome. Paul went to see them, and because he was a tent-maker as they were, he stayed and worked with them. (Acts 18:1–3)

1. What kind of work was this woman doing?

2. With whom did she work?

3. What details about the story interest you, and what do you wish you knew more about?

TABITHA

One final example to consider is that of Tabitha in Acts 9.

> In Joppa there was a disciple named Tabitha (in Greek her name is Dorcas); she was always doing good and helping the poor. About that time she became ill and died, and her body was washed and placed in an upstairs room. Lydda was near Joppa; so when the disciples heard that Peter was in Lydda, they sent two men to him and urged him, "Please come at once!" Peter went with them, and when he arrived he was taken upstairs to the room. All the widows stood round him, crying and showing him the robes and other clothing that Dorcas had made while she was still with them. Peter sent them all out of the room; then he got down on his knees and prayed. Turning toward the dead woman, he said, "Tabitha, get up." She opened her eyes, and seeing Peter she sat up. He took her by the hand and helped her to her feet. Then he called for the believers, especially the widows, and presented her to them alive. This became known all over Joppa, and many people believed in the Lord. (Acts 9:36–42)

1. What kind of work was this woman doing?

2. With whom did she work?

3. What details about the story interest you, and what do you wish you knew more about?

PART 2

Social Influence and Status

5

Patronage

O ne of the words Paul uses to describe Phoebe is "benefactor": "She has been a benefactor of many people, including me." There's a lot of evidence from the ancient world that can help us understand what this word signaled to Paul's first readers. Phoebe was a patron, something that was very common in the first century, both of men and of women.

Paul himself acts as a patron to Phoebe by introducing her to the congregation in Rome. Paul had never been to Rome at the time he wrote the letter, but he was already known to people there. He writes, "I ask you to receive her in the Lord in a way worthy of his people and to give her any help she may need from you" (Rom. 16:2). Paul uses his influence to introduce Phoebe and ensure that she will get a warm response.

What did patrons do? Ancient readers already knew the answer to that question, and they brought that knowledge with them when they read the New Testament texts. In our society, we also have patrons: you might be a patron of the arts, for example, by donating to a museum or buying season tickets to your city's orchestra. In the ancient world, patronage involved a wider range of actions, and it was more foundational to the way society functioned than it is today. So if we learn more about people's expectations of patrons, we will have a better idea of the kinds of things Phoebe—and other New Testament women—might have done.

The Various Acts of Patrons

Social interactions of the New Testament period were strongly shaped by patron/client relationships. In a nutshell, clients were people of lower status who made ties with patrons (of higher status) who could help them out. Patrons provided assistance, including things like making loans, securing business connections, writing letters of introduction, or lending their political influence. In return, clients showed honor to their patrons. Often, people were both patrons and clients: they made connections with some people who had higher social standing, but they also had social connections and influence to offer to those whose status was lower than theirs.

Most important, clients paid honor to their patrons, and honor was something people valued a great deal. Honoring someone was a way of highlighting the social standing of the person, and there were lots of ways to do it. For example, in personal interactions, clients showed honor through mannerisms that signaled deference to patrons. Clients visited patrons—a kind of social calling that showed honor. And, as we've seen many times already, people honored others with gifts, including inscriptions that publicly proclaimed the recipient's honor for all to see.

Let's consider the specific patronage of our characters, Marcus and Paula. While he was alive, Marcus was acknowledged as a good-natured person who liked to help others. He had a number of business associates and neighbors who would often visit him to maintain good relationships with him. Sometimes they would ask *Women played most of* him for help. For example, one man who trans-*the same roles as patrons* ported Marcus's crops to market lost his wagon in a *that men did.* fire, and Marcus loaned him money for a new one. The man paid Marcus back, and he also showed gratitude to Marcus, for example, by speaking kindly of Marcus to friends and neighbors, and always charging Marcus his best rates.

Now, you might think that Marcus would be the patron everyone would seek out. But remember that Paula also owned a productive farm. In fact, her orchards produced the best apples and dates in the region. Paula had a vendor who sold her produce in a nearby town, and when the vendor wanted to expand his sales, Paula wrote a letter of introduction to a cousin of hers who lived in the vendor's town. The vendor visited the cousin with the letter and ended up selling produce for both the cousin and a neighboring farm.

Relationships like these were essential to the functioning of ancient society. People made social alliances through which they helped one another, with the expectation that the other person would reciprocate. Upper-class people had money and connections to powerful people. Lower-class people didn't have those things to offer in return, but they could be faithful business partners and show loyalty to their patrons.

Women played most of the same roles as patrons that men did. One act of patronage was to offer a loan to a client who needed one. Some of the documents from Egypt record loans between women. For example, one papyrus from Egypt shows a legal agreement between two women who borrowed 372 drachmas from another woman.[1] In this case, the woman loaning money acted as a patron to the other two women.

Civic Patronage

People were patrons of cities or civic groups, not just of individuals. In this time period, cities relied on wealthier people to undertake projects that beautified the city and provided civic amenities including public baths, theaters, and the shows that were performed in them. Both men and women with property could become patrons of their cities by making such donations. Women's patronage was a natural extension of their ownership of property. Social norms encouraged those who had property to use it for the sake of their families and for the community at large. Both men and women acted as patrons and were rewarded with increased social standing in their communities.

Civic patronage also included roles as priests and gifts funding temples or festivals to the gods. There was no separation of church and state in New Testament times. Instead, religion was an important part of civic life, because the gods were understood to protect and benefit the city. A wealthy patron might serve as a priest, make donations that funded a yearly festival honoring a particular god, improve the temple buildings, or donate new ones. Lower-status people could also be patrons, only they might donate a portion of a mosaic floor for the temple rather than the whole thing. All of these gifts were seen not only as a form of religious devotion but also as a contribution to the civic good.

On a smaller scale, civic groups needed meeting places and smaller funds for whatever tasks they undertook. Many such groups supported the needs of their neighborhood, profession, or religion. Professional guilds, for example, organized efforts and promoted the well-being and social standing of their field. Often, associations would pool resources to honor deceased members of their community. Although women were only rarely listed as official members of these guilds, they were honored as supporters and occasionally as leaders.

Women with less money and social standing were patrons in their own ways.

We know of these donations now because the donor's name and gift were often etched on stones that survive. In fact, the inscription itself was one tangible way that communities and clients honored their patrons. Junia Rustica, Ummidia Quadratilla, and Claudia Metrodora are examples of this we have already seen, and there are many similar monuments from this period across the Roman Empire that honor both male and female donors. Many inscriptions praised grand projects undertaken by people with important civic and religious titles, and others recorded smaller gifts of less important people.

Flavia Ammon was a wealthy woman from Asia Minor who was part of the local elite. She was honored with this inscription: "The tribe of the Tethades to Flavia Ammon, daughter of Moschus, who is called

Aristion, high priestess of the temple of Asia in Ephesus, president, twice *stephanēphoros*, priestess of Massilia, president of the games, wife of Flavius Hermocrates, for her excellence and decorous life and her holiness."[2] Flavia held several municipal offices: the words "president" and *stephanēphoros* (a type of city magistrate) indicate this. She was also patron of the games and held two religious offices as well.

Many women with less money and social standing than Flavia were patrons in their own ways. For example, one inscription records the gift of a Jewish woman named Saprikia, who gave 150 feet of a mosaic.[3] And in Pompeii, some of the political posters supporting the elections of candidates were sponsored by women: "Caprasia along with Nymphius—her neighbors too—ask you to vote for Aulus Vettius Firmus for the aedileship; he is worthy of the office."[4] This endorsement appeared on the side of a wine shop. Caprasia was probably the proprietor there. While not a wealthy person, she used the influence and resources she had to accomplish her goals.

Many of the inscriptions honoring women patrons identify their roles with the same vocabulary used for men. For example, Flavia's roles of president and *stephanēphoros* were the same titles assigned to men. Women took on roles as magistrates, priests, and patrons, and were praised as pious and loyal to their cities.

However, some vocabulary for women is distinctive. For example, women were hailed as "mother of the assembly" or "daughter of the city." Although those particular titles were not held by men, they still convey the gratitude of the group for the important roles the women played in their community.

With all this in mind, let's return to Marcus and Paula's family to imagine how such patronage worked. Some months after Marcus died, Paula encouraged Marcella to put her name forward to serve as priest for a popular shrine in their town. As priest, Marcella would fund that year's festival celebrating the god's protection. She would sit at the head of a procession through the town and offer the initial sacrifice. By serving as priest, Marcella could establish her reputation as a civic-minded person who was loyal to her town.

Both men and women served as priests, and Marcus and Paula had both done so previously. The role of priest was chosen annually by a vote of the male citizens in the town. Marcella talked to her associates in the local brick-making guild, and they agreed to vote for her. They appreciated Marcella's generosity, and they knew that the attention the brick-makers would receive as a result of her priesthood would benefit them all.

Civic patronage was essential to the benefits ancient cities had to offer.

Marcella was elected, to the delight of her supporters and family. To celebrate, the brick-makers guild suggested an inscription be erected at the shrine, praising Marcella (and her father before her) for their dedication to the god. In return, Marcella offered to pay the expense of the inscription.

Civic patronage was essential to the benefits ancient cities had to offer. Patrons used their resources to build up the city, and they were honored with leadership positions and with public praise. Women and men both served as patrons during the New Testament period.

Women in Civic Leadership

The idea that women played these important roles in their cities may be surprising to us. We've usually heard that ancient women did not play public roles, and it's true that cultural norms typically assigned women to "household" tasks. However, ancient people would not have seen women's roles in the household as something that restricted their actions as civic leaders.

In the Roman period, what counted as "public" was actually a very narrow realm of legislative or judicial offices. It's true that women very rarely held these positions. However, commerce, political lobbying, and the use of social influence for the benefit of the city were *all* things ancient people considered "private." We've already seen how family business interests were part of the household realm that was deemed appropriate for women. It turns out that these roles as patrons were also understood as part of women's work. So an ancient person who saw Marcella's role as a priest and the inscription that honored her would not have understood her to have done anything that was unusual for women to do.

Although women were associated with the home, they weren't expected to stay hidden away there. "Public" and "private" were not words that designated the spaces where activities took place back then. Instead, "public" actions were those that were taken on behalf of the state, and "private" ones were taken on behalf of the individual or family. In fact, some actions that Romans defined as "public" actually took place in homes. And, as we've seen, some of the private interests required people to take care of business outside of the household itself.

Thus, civic patronage was an activity with which women were rightly concerned. This is counterintuitive to us today. For us, business and social or political influence are considered "public," but for the ancients, they were "private" matters. Such activities therefore fell into a category of action that was part of a woman's conventional domain.

Going forward, when we interpret New Testament texts about women, it will therefore help to avoid using the words "public" and "private" entirely. The words mean something so different now that they confuse rather than clarify. The assumption that women belonged to a narrow "private" sphere is a misunderstanding that can get in the way of acknowledging that women played the important roles we learn about from inscriptions. That's why I've been describing women's involvement as "civic" rather than "public."

The most important thing to remember is that women who filled these positions weren't breaking any rules. In fact, they were doing just what their communities hoped they would: they were using their social standing and wealth to benefit their city or civic group.

Patronage of New Testament Women

The first readers of the New Testament would have been familiar with these social patterns. We see something like a trade association at work in Acts 19, when the silversmiths of Ephesus worry that Paul's success in teaching will lead to fewer statues of Artemis. Their concern is not just for their own livelihood but also for their city, which was widely renowned for its temple to Artemis. Ancient readers of the story would have understood the social network that helped to unite the silversmiths in their outcry.

Early readers would also have understood the social roles women played as patrons. Women with wealth had influence in their communities. They held offices, often with the same titles men did, and their communities counted on their support. Lower-class women also served in less prestigious roles and gave gifts of smaller amounts. Early readers would have seen these ideas reflected in the descriptions of women in the New Testament.

For example, Bernice was a woman of high standing who appears at the end of Acts. She is traveling with a group of elite officials who hear Paul's testimony in Jerusalem. She's introduced this way: "After several days had passed, King Agrippa and Bernice arrived at Caesarea to welcome Festus" (Acts 25:13 NRSV). Festus was the newly appointed Roman governor of Judea. Bernice's brother, Herod Agrippa II, was the local ruler from 53 to 93 CE. Ancient readers would understand that this was an official state visit, smoothing relations between the local officials and the powerful Roman state. Although Bernice is not a government official, she is a person of very high status and sister to King Agrippa. Her presence added honor to the situation.

Bernice is worth mentioning in the story because she was a person of great wealth and high status. Ancient readers wouldn't have been surprised to see a woman like her present in the story at an official event. In fact, she is mentioned again in Acts 25:23 and in Acts 26:30–31, as a part of the group's warm response to Paul's words.

In many cases, the New Testament doesn't specify what kind of support women offer to the Jesus movement. Their involvement is mentioned, and early readers would have used their cultural knowledge to fill in the gaps. When we read these passages now, we also fill in details of the story with the historical information that we have available.

Read the following passages and use the questions to explore how ancient readers may have understood these women's actions.

WOMEN PATRONS OF JESUS'S PARTY

> After this, Jesus traveled about from one town and village to another, proclaiming the good news of the kingdom of God. The Twelve were with him, and also some women who had been cured of evil spirits and diseases: Mary (called Magdalene) from whom seven demons had come out; Joanna the wife of Chuza, the manager of Herod's household; Susanna; and many others. These women were helping to support them out of their own means. (Luke 8:1–3)

1. List the women involved and any details you can find about them.

2. List the words that describe the women's involvement as patrons.

3. Luke doesn't describe specifically what these women were doing. Based on your knowledge of patronage, how do you think readers from the time period would have understood these women's patronage activity?

Matthew provides this description of the scene at Jesus's crucifixion.

> Many women were there, watching from a distance. They had fol-
> lowed Jesus from Galilee to care for his needs. Among them were
> Mary Magdalene, Mary the mother of James and Joseph, and the
> mother of Zebedee's sons. (Matt 27:55–56)

1. List the women involved and any details you can find about them.

2. List the words that describe the women's involvement as patrons.

3. How do you think readers from the time period would have understood this activity?

Paul's letter mentions Phoebe as a patron, but it also serves as a letter
of recommendation for her as she travels to Rome.

> I commend to you our sister Phoebe, a deacon of the church in
> Cenchreae. I ask that you receive her in the Lord in a way worthy
> of his people and to give her any help she may need from you,
> for she has been the benefactor of many people, including me.
> (Rom. 16:1–2)

1. Which words in the passage suggest that Paul includes these
verses as a recommendation of Phoebe?

2. Which words describe Phoebe's own patronage?

3. How do you think readers from the time period would have understood this situation?

6

Social Influence

Phoebe was a "benefactor of many people, including [Paul]." In the last chapter we saw a range of things that patrons did. But how would the role of benefactor shape Phoebe's interactions with others in the church? What sort of power did patrons hold? We can learn more about Phoebe by considering the social implications of her role as benefactor.

Some interpreters have viewed Phoebe as a "helper" instead of a patron, and indeed the New American Standard Bible translates the Greek word (*prostatis*) that way. Although in its masculine form the word *prostatēs* clearly means patron, the translators' decision to render the feminine version, *prostatis*, as "helper" suggests that female patrons weren't really patrons, only helpers. The decision to translate the word in this way probably reflects the translators' misunderstanding of the kinds of roles women conventionally played. We've already seen many examples of women patrons, and in this chapter we'll examine the kind of authority these women had.

Patronage and Power

Patronage brought with it considerable social power. Patrons used their social standing to advocate for their family and their clients. Clients were tied to their patrons by social bonds that brought expectations of loyalty. So patrons had influence with people of their social class and also had a loyal client base to lend political support when needed.

The more honor patrons accrued through their gifts and festivals and loans, the more influence they had within their cities. The inscriptions and statues that recognized patrons were a visible symbol of their stature within the community. Those who were granted such honors had already used their authority to benefit others, and the inscription or statue made that authority manifest in a tangible way.

Wealthier patrons also exercised informal political power. Although women were not judges and were not allowed to vote in local assemblies, they could influence the proceedings—as men did—by talking to their allies about their opinions. To be sure, at the highest levels of Roman government, most of the authority was held by men. However, those men were also surrounded by high-ranking women who used their social standing to influence political and social events.

Patronage brought with it considerable social power.

As the wife of the first emperor, Livia carved out a prominent new role for herself as a patron. She gave gifts to the populace, including the dedication and renovation of temples. She also gave gifts to individuals and received clients in her home to hear their requests. The historian Dio Cassius wrote about the difficulty Livia's son, Tiberius, had when he became emperor due to the power of his mother.

> For she occupied a very exalted station, far above all women of former days, so that she could at any time receive the senate and such of the people as wished to greet her in her house. . . . The letters of Tiberius bore her name for a time, also, and communications were addressed to both alike. Except that she never ventured to enter the senate-chamber or the camps or the public assemblies, she undertook to manage everything as if she were sole ruler.[1]

Livia's power was unofficial but nonetheless real.

You might think that such power was limited to only a few women, and it's true that other women didn't have the wealth or clout of Livia. But women in other parts of the empire emulated Livia in her role as patron. Livia capitalized on the changes taking place in Roman society to craft a new kind of role for herself, but it was a role other women adopted as well. And the cities that benefited from women's gifts supported their participation and added to their stature by acknowledging their gratitude to them.

Most of the time, the influence of such patrons is not conveyed in the evidence that still exists. We can imagine

Livia's power was unofficial but nonetheless real.

such women at the head of a processional at an important festival or presiding at the theater or games. We can imagine how, seeing her stature in the community, others would approach her with a request to use her status to influence events. All of these were common roles patrons played.

But occasionally we do have direct evidence of this kind of influence. For example, one inscription praises the political advocacy of Junia Theodora, a citizen of Corinth and a contemporary of Phoebe and Paul. Junia probably grew up in the neighboring region of Lycia and moved to Corinth as an adult. But when her fellow countrymen were in political danger, they turned to her for help. Junia assisted them, and they honored her in five inscriptions in Corinth. Here's one:

> Greetings from the council and people of Myra to the magistrates of Corinth. Many of our citizens who travelled in your territory testified concerning a citizen of yours, Junia Theodora, daughter of Lucius, and the devotion and zeal which she used on their behalf, occupying herself continually for our people particularly at the time of their arrival in your city; this is why, according her our approval for her loyalty to the city, we hold her in the greatest es-

teem, and have decided at the same time to write to you as well in order that you may know of the gratitude of the city.[2]

This inscription identifies Junia's devotion to her people, but it doesn't say how she "occupied herself" on behalf of the people. From the other inscriptions, we learn that Junia assisted the Lycians in a time of political strife. She offered them refuge and exerted her influence on their behalf. They needed an important person to step up and help them, and Junia Theodora did. The city showed its gratitude by commissioning and paying for the inscriptions.

Women like Junia Theodora show the kind of social and political involvement that was likely expected of women patrons, just as it was of male patrons. These inscriptions are like the tip of an iceberg. They are what we can physically see after the centuries have elapsed. But the part we can no longer see—the larger part of the iceberg that lies beneath the water—is the considerable social and political power that these women had in their communities. Their influence and status in the community prompted the inscription that now remains visible to us.

Other ancient stories also give us a glimpse of the influence of high-standing women. The Roman historian Livy tells a story about women who turned out in the streets to advocate for the repeal of a law. (We'll talk more about that example in the chapters on speech and silence.) Livy describes a scene in which women spoke to senators about their position on legislation and succeeded in getting the law changed. This is probably an unusual example; it was more common for women to speak to individuals than to rally in the streets. But the use of influence to achieve political ends was not unusual for women.

Another example from Jewish tradition comes from the book of Judith. I mentioned Judith in chapters 1 and 3 because of the wealth she inherited. But along with that wealth came social influence. In the story, Judith's town is threatened by the Assyrian general Holofernes and his army. The town is cut off and in need of water, and the town's leader announces that he will surrender in five days unless God intervenes to help them. Judith is angry that the leaders are putting God to the test, and she summons them to her house and admonishes them. She subsequently saves the town from this danger. For our purposes, though, the point is that when Judith summons the town elders to her house, they go! And when she speaks, they acknowledge her wisdom. No one says, "Hey, who are you to talk to us that way?" or "It's none of your business!" As one of the leading women of the town, Judith has the social standing to influence its leaders.

Another striking example of legal persuasion comes from a second-century Christian text, the Acts of Paul and Thecla. Thecla's story was very popular among early Christ believers. It is the story of a young woman who became a follower of Paul. In fact, she was so devout that she broke off her engagement to pursue Paul's teachings on sexual self-control (cf. 1 Cor. 7). Thecla came from a prominent family, and her family and community viewed her refusal to marry as disloyalty. So her interest in Paul's teaching sparked a crisis. She was brought before the governor, but it was her mother, Theocleia, who pronounced the sentence: "Burn the lawless one! Burn the one who will not wed in the midst of the theater, so that all that the wives who have been taught by [Paul] will fear" (Acts of Paul and Thecla 20). The narrator states that the governor was disturbed about the case, but that he nevertheless went along with Theocleia's demands. Thecla was saved by God, who extinguished the fire with rain. Many readers are so astonished that a mother would react this way that it's easy to overlook the clear authority Theocleia had in determining the outcome of the legal proceedings.

Social Influence and Patronage

The power women exercised was not usually formal political power. We tend to focus only on whether women had access to such formal channels of political power because these are very important in our own context, and women and men fought for many years to secure access to the ballot box and the ability to run for office. But there are many informal ways people exercise power. And this was true for both men and women in the New Testament period. After all, only a small percentage of men were governors or kings. For most people, the kind of political and social influence that was available to them involved the use of their social status to forge connections between people.

Patrons used their social networks to influence others in order to improve their standing in business and politics, or to advocate for their friends and clients. The tangible benefit of using one's power in this way was honor: patrons were owed deference by those they served, and the many statues erected in the period were concrete manifestations of the social honor patrons accrued. Women pursued honor alongside men.

Women pursued honor alongside men.

Patronage and Influence in the New Testament

One New Testament episode in which we see the political influence of a woman character is the story of John the Baptist's death. John had criticized Herod's marriage to his brother's ex-wife. Matthew tells the story this way:

> Now Herod had arrested John and bound him and put him in prison because of Herodias, his brother Philip's wife, for John had been saying to him, "It is not lawful for you to have her." Herod wanted to kill John, but he was afraid of the people, because they considered John a prophet. On Herod's birthday the daughter of Herodias danced for the guests and pleased Herod so much that he promised with an oath to give her whatever she asked. Prompted by her mother, she said, "Give me here on a platter the head of John the Baptist." The king was distressed, but because of his oaths and his dinner guests, he ordered that her request be granted, and had John beheaded in the prison. His head was brought on a platter and given to the girl, who carried it to her mother. (Matt. 14:3–11)

Herodias didn't hold the formal political power required to execute John herself. However, she was a woman of high status, and she used the access that power gave her to influence events. In this case, she saw Herod's offer to her daughter as an opportunity to seek revenge against John, and so she asked for John's death.

Few women had the elite status of Herodias. But other women also used the social status and resources they had—and often used them for good instead of for ill. In the previous chapter, we studied passages in which women are mentioned as patrons of the Jesus movement. Let's look at two of them again and think about the ways that the English translations can emphasize, diminish, or even hide the influence of these women.

THE WOMEN WHO PROVIDED FOR JESUS

Luke 8 describes a group of women who provided for Jesus and the disciples, naming some of them.

> After this, Jesus traveled about from one town and village to another, proclaiming the good news of the kingdom of God. The Twelve were with him, and also some women who had been cured of evil spirits and diseases: Mary (called Magdalene) from whom seven demons had come out; Joanna the wife of Chuza, the manager of Herod's household; Susanna; and many others. These women were helping to support them out of their own means. (Luke 8:1–3)

Sometimes the words in these passages are translated differently. The word translated "helping to support" in the NIV, above, is the Greek word *diakoneō*, which means to serve. It's related to the noun from which we get the word "deacon." The text doesn't specify what kind of support the women supply, although it does say they do so "out of their own means." Some translations state that the women "ministered to" or "provided for" Jesus.

Here are some examples of translations of Luke 8:3:

NIV: "Joanna the wife of Chuza, the manager of Herod's household; Susanna; and many others. These women were helping to support them out of their own means."

NRSV: "Joanna, the wife of Herod's steward Chuza, and Susanna, and many others, who provided for them out of their resources."

KJV: "Joanna the wife of Chuza Herod's steward, and Susanna, and many others, which ministered unto him of their substance."

1. Circle or underline the translation differences that seem important.

2. Do you think the word choice makes a difference in these verses? If so, how do you think it affects the way readers today understand these women's roles?

3. If your personal Bible is a different translation from the ones provided here, look up this verse and write it down here.

4. Based on what you understand about the historical situation, which seems like the better word choice to you?

PHOEBE THE DEACON

In Romans 16:1, Paul describes Phoebe as a *diakonos* of the church in Cenchreae, which is translated in the NIV as "deacon." Some translations render it as "servant." In verse 2, she is a "benefactor of many," including Paul. Some versions translate this portion as a "helper of many."

NIV: "I commend to you our sister Phoebe, a deacon, of the church in Cenchreae. I ask you to receive her in the Lord in a way worthy of his people and to give her any help she may need from you, for she has been the benefactor of many people, including me."

NRSV: "I commend to you our sister Phoebe, a deacon of the church at Cenchreae, so that you may welcome her in the Lord as is fitting for the saints, and help her in whatever she may require from you, for she has been a benefactor of many and of myself as well."

NASB: "I commend to you our sister Phoebe, who is a servant of the church which is at Cenchrea; that you receive her in the Lord in a manner worthy of the saints, and that you help her in whatever matter she may have need of you; for she herself has also been a helper of many, and of myself as well."

1.   Circle or underline the translation differences that seem important.

2.   Do you think the word choice makes a difference in these verses? If so, say how you think it affects the way readers today understand these women's roles.

3.   If your personal Bible is a different translation from the ones provided here, look up this verse and write it down here.

4.   Based on what you understand about the historical situation, which seems like the better word choice to you?

7

Education

P hoebe was probably the person who carried Paul's letter to Rome. It was common for letter writers to recommend the traveler who carried the letter, introducing them to people at their destination who could give them a place to stay or help them carry out their business. Many interpreters wonder whether Phoebe read the letter aloud to the church in Rome. This also would fit cultural patterns of the time, but it would require Phoebe to be fairly well educated. How likely was that in this period of time? This chapter explores patterns of women's education.

Literacy and Education

The question of whether women and girls were educated is connected to the bigger question of how many people could read and write. If lots of people were literate, then it seems more likely that women would learn too. But if only a few elite men were, then most women were probably illiterate. So let's start by thinking about whether people in general were educated.

Literacy rates are notoriously difficult to determine in the New Testament period. There isn't much evidence to go on, and some of it is conflicting or unclear. One reason it's hard to tell how many people could read and write is that it was common to use a scribe to write for you. This didn't mean the author couldn't read or write, however. Even educated people—like Paul himself—dictated their letters to a scribe. They also used scribes to draw up business contracts or loans, because scribes knew the specific wording to use that made the agreement legal. When wealthy people employed a scribe, we can therefore be fairly certain it wasn't because they couldn't write.

But lower-class people also used scribes to write letters or draw up documents. In their cases, it's more difficult to tell whether the sender was literate. Sometimes senders would write the final greeting of the letter themselves, which makes it clear that they could write, at least a little. Sometimes the handwriting is wobbly, and it seems likely the person writing didn't have much practice.

Some aspects of the historical record suggest that literacy rates were very low. For example, in a number of legal documents, one or both parties had another person sign for them because they were illiterate. One document described the agreement for the apprenticeship of an enslaved girl, Taorsenouphis, owned by a woman named Segathis. Neither Segathis nor the weaver to whom she apprenticed her slave wrote their own names. Both parties brought a trusted individual with them to sign the contract. The wording used by each signer was similar: "I, Pausiris, son of Panephremis, acknowledge that I have received the girl to learn the craft for the aforementioned period of time and I shall do each of the specified things." Then his proxy wrote below that "I, Satabous, have written on his behalf since he is illiterate."[1] Legal documents like this one that were signed by a second party suggest that many people couldn't write, or couldn't write well enough to complete the process themselves.

However, a number of cultural factors also make it seem that education was more common than we might think. For one thing, legal documents were often written in Greek. But people often spoke another local language as their first language. Perhaps Pausiris (from our example above) could write his name in Egyptian but not in Greek. He may even have understood spoken Greek but could not write

Greek letters. So, even though the word "illiteracy" is used, it may only describe his inability to write Greek.

Another thing that suggests higher rates of literacy is that writing was important to people, regardless of their social class. Writing was ubiquitous and played important roles in people's religious, social, and economic lives. For example, many temples were covered with writing. Whole areas of the walls or pillars of a shrine might be covered with messages. Other temples had a place for people to leave prayers written on paper and rolled up. Some of the messages written on temples thank the deity for healing received. Others record the fulfillment of a vow someone made to the god. All of these were important moments in people's religious lives, and the fact that they involved written words underscores the importance of writing.

People also used receipts—just as we do today—as proof that they had paid for something or had received the goods that were promised. If Pausiris loaned you money and you paid him back, but then the next week he forgot and claimed that you hadn't, it would be a headache for both of you, right? So people wrote down important transactions. Examples of this that we've already seen (in chapters 1 and 3) were legal documents recording the items in a woman's dowry—or verifying that they had been returned to her.

All this suggests that writing was important and a regular part of people's lives. But it's not always possible to say with any certainty who was doing all this writing. Did individuals add their own prayers of thanksgiving to temple walls, or did a friend do it for them? Or did they pay a scribe to do so? Did shopkeepers write their own receipts, or did they have another person do it for them? Could people read the tax receipts they got, or did they just trust that they were correct? The evidence we have does not usually allow us to answer these questions.

Writing was important and a regular part of people's lives.

But it does seem that the quantity of writing that survives points to the important role it played for people. And that suggests that many people were literate—or at least had some literacy skills. If you were a shopkeeper, for example, you probably needed to know some basic math and have some reading skills. You had to be able to tabulate a customer's bill, and you probably needed a system to keep track of supplies and inventory. You didn't need to compose a political speech or read Aristotle. So you weren't fully literate, but you had enough education to do what your job required.

Quite a bit of writing also seems to come from lower-class people. This is the writing least likely to survive, but we catch glimpses of it—for example, in the graffiti of Pompeii, preserved by the volcanic ash that covered it for centuries. Some people posted political notices touting their favorite candidate for office. Others wrote informal recommendations, a sort of advertisement of services. Like our graffiti today, some messages were vulgar, and many were declarations of love. Some were bits of wisdom or quotations. Some seem to be by people practicing writing the alphabet. The location and content of some of these scrawlings suggest that many were not written by the elite. For example, a notice outside a tavern frequented by the lower classes seems likely to have been written by one of its customers.

All this writing also suggests an audience who could read it. Why promote a political candidate in writing if none of the electorate can read? Or why advertise the next gladiatorial games? Of course, some passersby could have asked a friend or a stranger to read the announcements to them. But the notices only make sense if we assume that a proportion of the target audience could read.

Another reason to think literacy rates were higher than we have imagined is that education had important social value. Being educated was a sign of status. And just as people sought honor through acts of patronage, they also sought to increase their social standing by educating their children. Children who were educated could have more opportunities for advancement than their parents did, but the fact of their literacy also brought increased standing in the eyes of others.

Although scholars debate the percentage of people who were educated, the actual number isn't very important for our purposes.

The essential thing to know is that people tried to achieve the level of education they needed for their job and their social standing. A shopkeeper needed some writing and basic math but didn't need much more. Elite people needed a high level of education. Even if they owned slaves to keep their records and write their letters, social norms required that they be able to discuss literature and grammar, and that men be trained to speak eloquently. These activities were a badge of one's status. There were also plenty of people—fishermen, bricklayers, farmhands, day laborers—who didn't need any education at all.

Women and Education

We have the same problems discerning literacy rates among women as we do in general. Women also employed scribes to write for them, but that doesn't tell us anything about their abilities. Many examples of writing don't have names attached, so there's no way to tell the gender of the writer.

Most of the lengthy works that still exist from the period were written by men. That fact doesn't tell us whether women could write, though it does suggest that their writings were not as valuable to those who copied and preserved them through all these years. If men's writing was more valuable, that supports the notion that they were more likely to be educated than women. This still doesn't tell us anything about whether women were illiterate. It just suggests they may have been less educated than men, or less likely to use their education to write history and philosophy.

The evidence suggests that the pattern for women's literacy was similar to the population at large. Women were educated to the extent they needed to be. As with men, that "need" was both economic and social. Literary skills were important both for one's job and to signify social status.

Taken as a whole, women were less likely than men to receive an education. A woman of the same social class as a man had lower status than he did, simply because of her gender. And inscriptions recording occupations show that women were less likely to fill clerical positions and roles that required more learning. Both of these facts suggest that people would have perceived less of a need for women to be educated.

But there were plenty of jobs women did in which literary skills would have been useful. As we saw in chapter 4, women were shopkeepers and needed to keep records. They were midwives, who would have benefited from reading medical books. They were even teachers themselves.

Women's education was also a way to display their family's social status—and a means to increase that status. An elite woman might be expected to attend dinner parties and discuss poetry or history. One first-century satirist, Juvenal, complains about women who seem to know the fine points of grammar better than the men around them! Juvenal's words reinforce the notion that people regarded it as problematic for a woman to upstage a man of high standing. However, the assumption that women had this kind of knowledge is also built into the picture Juvenal paints for his reader. And women achieved that level of learning because their families saw the social benefits of their daughters being able to display their education.

Poorer families also benefited from a daughter's education. A girl who was educated could do a better job working for her family. Roman law acknowledged that girls could be in charge of shops. A girl with some literacy skills would be a good candidate for that kind of work. In addition, if the girl could read and write and other family members could not, she could help them with letters and legal documents.

Education could also help the daughter to marry a man of higher status than if she had been illiterate. For a wealthy woman, education was both a sign of the good breeding that was expected of the elite and evidence that she could raise children to be similarly refined. For a lower-class woman, literacy skills would demonstrate her greater capacity to work for the benefit of the family. For every social class, a better marriage was important to the girl involved, because it could increase her own social standing. A good match was also useful to her family for the social connections it would bring. If a family could afford it, educating girls made a lot of sense.

So again, the best conclusion seems to be that people educated their children to the extent that they could afford and in ways that were useful for their situation in life. Women were typically less likely than men to receive an education, and when they did, they were not as highly educated as their male peers. But many did still learn to read and write. They used those skills in their livelihoods and passed them on to their children.

Girls and boys were educated in the same schools and with the same curriculum, at least through age fourteen or so. There is no evidence that single-sex education was common in antiquity, but there was a bias toward boys. For example, all the textbooks use boys as illustrations rather than girls, imagining the typical student as a boy. Yet girls learned in those classrooms and from those "typical" student examples just as boys did.

Some of the specific evidence we have for girls' education comes from funeral monuments. One commemorates an eight-year-old girl named Magnilla, who was "learned beyond her years." The idea that Magnilla's parents chose these words to honor her after her death conveys the importance of being educated and the social status it brought—even at eight years old! Another has a picture of a boy and a girl standing on either side of their teacher. Other pictures depict girls and women holding books in their hands.

Girls and boys were educated in the same schools and with the same curriculum.

A few letters from Egypt refer to girls in school. One letter from the family of a girl named Heraidous requests that another family member send a gift for her teacher "so that he may put in much effort for her."[2] Another note from the same family asks for a book for Heraidous to read.

A few women achieved a high education by the standards of their day. One woman named Sulpicia authored love poems. Another,

Timoxena, who was married to the philosopher Plutarch, wrote her own philosophical treatise. Plutarch commended it to his former student, a young woman named Eurydice, for whom he also composed a treatise on marriage.

Other evidence shows that some educated women served as teachers. Cornelia was a famous Roman woman who was applauded for her work in educating her sons. Other elite women oversaw the education of their children. Even if some did so by employing a tutor, the task of supervising the children's education required enough knowledge to discern what should be taught and whether it was done well.

Other women were teachers in the more formal sense: parents paid them to educate their children. One letter from a woman to her husband in the military assures him that the children are well and taking classes from a woman teacher. Another letter from a woman, Serapias, to her children, sends them greetings from "Athenais the teacher." A painted mummy portrait identifies the deceased as Hermione, a secondary-school teacher.

Most of the time, in graffiti and letters, the gender of the author is unknown. But sometimes we see clues that women were writers. Some women penned the closing greeting on their letters. For example, one woman appended a simple "Farewell" to a letter written by a scribe. Another woman signed her own marriage contract: "I Thais, have sworn the oath written above and I shall do as prescribed."[3]

A few of the letters that still exist seem to have been written entirely by the female sender. For example, this one was written by a woman in the Egyptian city of Philadelphia:

Thermouthas to Valerias her mother, very many greetings and always good health. I received from Valerius the basket with 20 pairs of wheat cakes and 10 pairs of loaves. Send me the blankets at the current price and nice wool, 4 fleeces. Give these to Valerius. And at the moment I am 7 months pregnant. And I salute Artemis and

little Nikarous and Valerius my lord—I long for him in my mind—
and Dionysia and Demetrous many times and little Taesis many
times and everyone in the house. And how is my father? Please,
send me news because he was ill when he left me. I salute nurse.
Rodine salutes you. I have set her to the handiwork; again I need
her, but I am happy.[4]

One reason to suggest that this may have been Thermouthas's own
writing is that the penmanship doesn't seem very practiced. She
was nonetheless able to write the whole letter and express what she
wanted to say.

New Testament Women and Education

Few New Testament passages contain any clues about the education
levels achieved by those mentioned. We don't get many more clues
about men's literacy than we do about women's. Paul was clearly an
educated person. Although he dictated his letters to a scribe, their
careful composition suggests a high level of education. Luke's Gospel
explicitly presents Jesus as one who could read—he stands up in the
synagogue to read from the prophet Isaiah (Luke 4:16–20). And in
the story of Jesus and the woman accused of adultery (John 7:53–
8:11), Jesus writes on the ground using his finger—presumably writing
words, although the story doesn't specify. The Gospels give us no
information about the education levels of the disciples.

Women characters are similarly opaque. But we can use the details of the story and what is known about ancient education to make
some inferences. John's version of Mary and Martha portrays them
as women who were likely to be literate, for example. The crowd that
gathers with the sisters after Lazarus's death may suggest they are a
family of some importance. They also have enough wealth and social
status to give a dinner party celebrating Lazarus's raising, with Jesus
and others in attendance. Mary owns a jar of perfume worth three

hundred denarii, which she uses to anoint Jesus's feet. As John portrays them, the family seems likely to be educated in accordance with their social status.

Phoebe also seems likely to have been educated. Paul's introduction of her includes her title in the Cenchreae church and notes her patronage, not just of Paul but of many others. This suggests that Phoebe had some wealth and therefore may also have been literate. In addition, Phoebe comes from the thriving city of Cenchreae, which, along with Corinth, formed an important passage for commerce from the Adriatic to the Aegean Sea. So she lived in a place where education was readily available. Chances are good, then, that Phoebe was literate and may have read the letter that she carried to the church in Rome.

Use the ideas of this chapter to explore the idea of literacy and education in the passages below.

THE CHARGE AGAINST JESUS

All four Gospels state that the Romans placed the charge against Jesus on his cross: "This is Jesus, the King of the Jews" (Matt. 27:37; cf. Mark 15:26; Luke 23:38; John 19:19).

1. Why do you think the Romans did so? Who did they expect to read the sign?

2. Matthew and Luke both describe the women disciples standing at a distance and watching (Matt. 27:55–56; Luke 23:49). Imagine yourself as one of these women. Can you read the inscription on the cross?

3. John emphasizes the importance of this inscription. He says, "Many of the Jews read this sign, for the place where Jesus was

crucified was near the city, and the sign was written in Aramaic, Latin and Greek" (John 19:20). What does John's language imply about literacy?

LYDIA AND PAUL

Luke tells the story of Lydia's encounter with Paul in Acts 16:11–15:

> From Troas we put out to sea and sailed straight for Samothrace, and the next day we went on to Neapolis. From there we traveled to Philippi, a Roman colony and the leading city of that district of Macedonia. And we stayed there several days. On the Sabbath we went outside the city gate to the river, where we expected to find a place of prayer. We sat down and began to speak to the women who had gathered there. One of those listening was a woman from the city of Thyatira named Lydia, a dealer in purple cloth. She was a worshiper of God. The Lord opened her heart to respond to Paul's message. When she and the members of her household were baptized, she invited us to her home. "If you consider me a believer in the Lord," she said, "come and stay at my house." And she persuaded us.

1. List the aspects of the story that might be indirect clues about Lydia's education level.

2. We'll never know for sure, but what would you guess about Lydia's literacy?

PART 3

Virtues of Women

8

Modesty

Paul doesn't say anything directly about Phoebe's virtue. But he does "commend" her to the church in Rome. And since he spent the previous four chapters of Romans giving instructions on how to live a Christian life, we have a pretty good idea of Paul's expectations. It seems likely that Phoebe was not only a patron but someone commendable—a person who lived the life of faith.

The picture that we've pieced together so far of Phoebe—as a property owner, patron, and educated person—may contradict our ideas of what ancient people considered a "good woman." Perhaps you're wondering why Phoebe wouldn't be expected to act in a more subservient manner. Weren't women supposed to spend their lives supporting men? And wouldn't that be especially true of someone who was considered a "good woman"? How could Phoebe (or any woman) be both virtuous and a leader?

These are really good questions! In the previous chapters, we've seen women managing their property and serving their communities as civic leaders. Some of that activity may seem to contradict what we have previously understood to be the ancient feminine ideal of silence and submission. We have a sense that women were supposed to defer to their husbands, but then we see women who are property owners and civic leaders in their own

How could Phoebe (or any woman) be both virtuous and a leader?

7

right. How were they considered virtuous if they also acted independently? If we want to understand what behavior was appropriate for women, it will help to think more about the feminine virtues.

The Feminine Ideal

The words used to describe the ideal woman are actually very consistent over many centuries. The ideal of a virtuous woman was one who was modest, industrious, and loyal to her family. Modern readers often imagine this profile as constraining women, thinking they had to stay at home and do whatever their husbands told them to do. That's not quite the case, as we shall see.

Let's start with some examples of women who are praised for traditional virtues. One burial inscription records a lengthy funeral speech given by Turia's husband at her death. Because he was wealthy enough to have the whole speech inscribed in stone, we get a detailed sense of what Turia did that was praiseworthy.

Some of the husband's language simply describes Turia as conforming to the classic feminine ideal: "Why should I mention your personal virtues—your modesty, obedience, affability, and good nature, your tireless attention to wool-working, your performance of religious duties without superstitious fear, your artless elegance and simplicity of dress?"[1] This description portrays Turia as an ideal wife: she is modest, industrious, and loyal to her family.

The ideal of a virtuous woman was one who was modest, industrious, and loyal to her family.

Here's an excerpt from a funeral inscription that a son erected to honor his mother, Murdia: "My dearest mother deserved greater praise than all others, since in modesty, propriety, chastity, obedience, wool-working, industry, and loyalty she was on an equal level with other good women, nor did she take second place to any woman in virtue, work and wisdom in times of danger."[2] Murdia's son praises her using these classic feminine ideals.

The adjectives used to describe Turia and Murdia were commonly found in inscriptions commemorating women. They give us a sense of the agreed-upon social norms of the time. These attributes were invariably mentioned when someone wanted to praise a woman and say how amazing she was.

Even though the words that described women's virtues stayed the same, what those attributes looked like in practice changed quite a lot over time. In the New Testament period, these feminine virtues often described *Self-control was both a male* women who were doing things that might *and female virtue.* surprise us. Virtuous women pursued their
economic and social interests and took on civic roles. This chapter explores what it meant for women in the New Testament period to fulfill the first of those classic feminine attributes, modesty. (In the next two chapters, we'll explore industry and loyalty, and then we'll look at ideal marital relationships.)

Modesty

Modesty was a complex virtue in antiquity. Today, we might think a woman is being modest if she dresses in a way that doesn't show too much of her body, or if she defers to other people around her. In the New Testament period, modesty could similarly describe one's dress or one's actions, but in either case it meant something different from what it means today.

The Greek word (*sōphrosynē*) that is often translated "modesty" also means "self-control." This definition is more useful in under-standing the virtue when it's attributed to women. The modest or self-controlled person was someone who prioritized the needs of their household or city over personal pleasures. Self-control was both a male and a female virtue, and in both cases the emphasis on self-discipline was the same.

MODEST DRESS

Just as today, modesty was an attribute that applied to the way people dressed. But here's the big difference: for us, modest dress is more about how much or little of one's body is showing. In the New Testament period, modesty in dress pointed to simple (as opposed to lavish) attire. So, if I were a wealthy Roman woman who owned pearls, gold, and expensive fabrics but I wore plainer clothes and only a simple necklace, that would be considered modest dress.

Figure 2. *Portrait bust of a priestess; Michael C. Carlos Museum, Emory University; photo by Bruce M. White, 2010*

As we've seen, this was a period of prosperity for many people. Few people were fabulously wealthy, but many people had some extra money to spend, and most people lived above the subsistence level. Because of the relative prosperity of the time, many people could display their wealth through jewelry, expensive fabrics, and elaborate hairstyles. Figure 2 shows a statue of a priestess with her hair done in one of the popular fashions.

Ancient writers were aware that such extravagance could conflict with other important social values. If wealthy people only spent their riches on elaborate dinner parties, they wouldn't have resources for the building projects that their cities relied upon them to fund. Individuals and families had reason to display their wealth to gain honor, but society also depended upon people donating great sums for the public good.

Because lavish dress could divert household resources, simple dress indicated self-control. It expressed wise judgment about the use of communal resources. At the heart of the ideal is the notion of self-discipline for the public good. Both men and women could display this virtue through their attire.

The philosopher Plutarch said this of the importance of modest dress for women: "What adorns a woman is what makes her better ordered—not gold nor emerald nor scarlet, but whatever gives an impression of dignity, discipline, and modesty."[3] For Plutarch and others of his time, being simply dressed meant one was adorned with virtue rather than riches.

MODEST SEXUAL BEHAVIOR

Sexual restraint was also an aspect of modesty. For a woman, sexual modesty meant having sex only with her husband. This was socially valuable because it ensured that her children were her husband's rightful heirs.

This kind of modesty was regarded as a form of self-control. Like anger or greed, the passion of sexual desire was something philosophers warned about. They understood that it was easy to get carried away by desire, thinking that fulfilling this need was the most important thing. But they taught that giving in to sexual desire would not bring true happiness. To be faithful to one's spouse, then, required control over one's passions. And women were generally expected to exhibit such virtue.

As you may expect, the standards for men were not quite as high. Philosophy aside, society gave men more freedom to pursue other sexual partners. Prostitution was a thriving business. Male slave owners also forced their slaves (male or female) to have sex. For men, the only strong disapproval came from having sex with a married woman. In general, society gave men greater sexual license.

However, philosophers of the day likewise encouraged men to show sexual restraint, and doing so was evidence of one's virtue. Plutarch contrasted the self-controlled husband with men who "have

the intemperate, pleasure-loving natures of dogs or goats."[4] He encouraged husbands not to associate with other women because of the
pain it would bring their wives. Nevertheless, he acknowledged that
it was common for men to have sex outside of marriage.

So, in the case of sexual modesty, women were held to a higher
standard than men. There are plenty of stories of women having affairs (though it's hard to tell how many of those stories are true).
But overall, the ancient sources give the impression that sexual in-
dulgence was much more common among men than women. Social
expectations helped to channel women's sexual practices toward the
exhibition of modesty.

MODESTY AS A CIVIC VIRTUE

We think of modesty as an individual virtue. Modesty affects one's
character or one's interactions with other people. We would be unlikely to consider an individual's modesty as something that was valuable to the community or the city. For Romans, however, self-control
was an important virtue, particularly among civic leaders.

Plutarch saw modesty as an important leadership quality. In the
same paragraph in which he advocated women being adorned with
virtue rather than finery, he told a story about a leader who received
a bunch of fancy clothes for his daughters—a nice gift *except* for one
problem: they came from a tyrant. The leader showed good judgment
in sending back the gifts. He said, "These ornaments will dishonor
me more than they will adorn my daughters."[5] The leader
Modesty was a recognized that being attracted to riches could lead him
civic responsibility. into an alliance with a tyrant, and that this could be bad
for his city. So resisting fancy dress is a sign that one has
the best interests of one's people at heart.

There were political and social reasons why people of this time
saw a connection between domestic virtues and civic leadership. The
Roman form of government had shifted from a more democratic rule
in the republican era to rule by an emperor. To support this shift,

the emperor and his allies drew on traditional values to portray the emperor as someone who exhibited virtues like self-control. They wanted to convey that the emperor truly was looking out for the country's well-being and wasn't simply a tyrant. The emphasis on self-control in this time period may have opened up additional space for women's civic participation, because self-control (or modesty) was already established as a feminine virtue.

People also understood sexual modesty as an important civic virtue. Strong marriages were seen as the bedrock of the social fabric. This was true in a practical sense—strong households contributed to the prosperity of the city. And husbands and wives who cultivated virtues like self-control made for strong households. In addition, people understood sexual fidelity as something that was pleasing to the gods. Faithful spouses honored the gods with their actions, and the gods in turn protected the city from war, famine, and the like.

So, although modesty was certainly an individual trait, it was also a civic responsibility. Those who dressed modestly displayed their wise judgment and willingness to contribute to the public good. Those who were sexually modest secured the well-being of the city by creating strong households and pleasing the gods.

This social and political context helps to explain how some women were praised for modesty even as they pursued a political agenda. Modesty or self-control connected traditional household virtues with the capacity for civic leadership. The same judgment needed to sustain a stable household also formed the foundation of a stable society.

Active and Virtuous Women

Modern scholars have often asserted that females who took on roles as patrons were exceptional women, and that other people saw them as renegades. But there's little evidence that women who did these things were understood as stepping outside of cultural conventions. Instead, the social definition of modesty supported women's participation in civic roles.

Women asserted their modesty at the same time that they undertook acts of civic patronage and leadership. Livia, the wife of Caesar Augustus, for example, took on an important civic role even as she was

Modesty supported women's participation in civic roles.

characterized as having traditional domestic virtues. Livia was a powerful patron in Rome and asserted her political influence. She also set an example that other women across the Roman Empire cited as they asserted their own influence as patrons. Yet authors praised Livia for having traditional virtues.

A number of inscriptions show that the women honored were not viewed as violating traditional norms of behavior in their leadership. In fact, many are praised both for traditional virtues and for being leaders of the city. The following example refers to the same Junia Theodora I discussed in chapter 6: "The people of Patara have decreed: since Junia Theodora, a Roman, living at Corinth, a woman of the greatest honor, living modestly, who is a friend of the Lycians and has dedicated her life to earning the gratitude of all the Lycians, has bestowed numerous benefits also on many of our citizens." The Lycians honored Junia for her influence on behalf of her people. But notice also how she is praised for "living modestly."

Junia's leadership in her community was not considered immodest. She was praised both for leadership and for traditional feminine virtue. Within her context, she did not appear to be breaking the rules of culture. She was doing something that was expected of a virtuous person. Her action did not contradict her virtue but confirmed it. Notice that a conventional virtue like modesty did not cancel out the active participation of women in society.

Modesty in the New Testament

This connection between wise judgment and self-control is one reason why people in the New Testament period did not experience women's leadership as contradicting social norms. Women who were identified as "modest" or self-controlled were exhibiting a virtue that was already associated with leadership. We see similar virtues expressed in a number of New Testament passages.

The Greek word for self-control or modesty appears occasionally in the New Testament writings. In 1 Timothy 2:8–15, for example, this word is found at the beginning and end of the instructions regarding women in worship. Here are the first two verses of that passage: "Women should dress themselves modestly (*sōphrosynē*) and decently in suitable clothing, not with their hair braided, or with gold, pearls, or expensive clothes, but with good works, as is proper for women who profess reverence for God" (1 Tim. 2:9–10 NRSV).

As you can see, the context of 1 Timothy supports the idea of modesty as self-control with regard to the use of household resources. In chapter 9, I take up the following verses of 1 Timothy that exhort women to be silent. The control of the tongue in certain social situations was also evidence of self-control (vv. 11–12). But I want to set aside that important topic for the moment to focus on other aspects of self-control or modesty.

Women who were identified as "modest" were exhibiting a virtue already associated with leadership.

In its historical context, *sōphrosynē* conveyed the self-control required of Christian leaders. As a whole, 1 Timothy 2:9–15 reflected conventional views. It upheld self-control in the wise use of household resources, as seen in the restraint shown through simple dress. Such restraint was consistent with the expectations for leadership in civic and religious groups in this period.

Later in the same letter, the author characterizes leaders within this community by the same virtues: "Now the overseer must be above reproach, faithful to his wife, temperate, self-controlled, respectable, hospitable, able to teach, not given to drunkenness, not violent but gentle, not quarrelsome, not a lover of money. He must manage his own family well and see that his children obey him, and he must do so in a manner worthy of full respect" (1 Tim. 3:2–4). The word translated "self-controlled" is the same Greek word we've been discussing (*sōphrōn*). It conveys someone who exhibits modesty or self-control. The passage affirms an important value in the culture, that those who were sought out for leadership positions should be people who look out for the common good.

Use the instructions below to explore how leaders were expected to express self-control.

BISHOPS

Reread the passage about bishops.

> Now the overseer must be above reproach, faithful to his wife, temperate, self-controlled, respectable, hospitable, able to teach, not given to drunkenness, not violent but gentle, not quarrelsome, not a lover of money. He must manage his own family well and see that his children obey him, and he must do so in a manner worthy of full respect. (1 Tim. 3:2–4)

Think about how the qualities listed here relate to the virtue of modesty/self-control. Fill in the chart below, describing what kind of self-control is indicated by these words.

Quality . . .	Shows control over . . .
Faithful to his wife (v. 2)	
Not given to drunkenness (v. 3)	
Not violent but gentle (v. 3)	
Not quarrelsome (v. 3)	
Not a lover of money (v. 3)	

DEACONS

Both male and female deacons were qualified for office with the same set of virtues.

> In the same way, deacons are to be worthy of respect, sincere, not indulging in much wine, and not pursuing dishonest gain. They must keep hold of the deep truths of the faith with a clear conscience. They must first be tested; and then if there is nothing against them, let them serve as deacons. In the same way, the women are to be worthy of respect, not malicious talkers but temperate and trustworthy in everything. (1 Tim. 3:8–11)

Most scholars today agree that it is likely that "women" in verse 11 refers to women deacons. In Greek, the wording makes a parallel between the overseers (v. 3), deacons (v. 8), and women (v. 11). Our Phoebe as well as many other sources indicate that women were deacons throughout the early church period. So it makes the most sense to see these women as deacons.

Notice how the qualifications for women deacons parallel those of men:

Men (v. 8)	Women (v. 11)
worthy of respect	worthy of respect
sincere	not malicious talkers
not indulging in much wine	temperate
not pursuing dishonest gain	trustworthy in all things

Think about how the qualities describing deacons and women deacons relate to the virtue of self-control. Fill in the chart, identifying the qualities you think are related to self-control and then stating the kind of self-control each quality indicates.

Quality...	Shows control over...

The language of 1 Timothy reflects a social context in which women who were honored for being self-controlled could still exercise various forms of leadership in their households and communities. This historical context should shape our understanding of 1 Timothy. It was common to see women in leadership roles who also fulfilled the social rules of modesty. Modesty did not simply limit women's leadership; it was also seen as the basis of good leadership.

9

Industry

Phoebe was a deacon and benefactor, but also someone "commendable." In the previous chapter we saw one reason why a person like Phoebe could have these important roles in her community and still be understood as a woman with classic feminine virtues. In this chapter, we'll continue to explore how early readers of the New Testament could have seen Phoebe's leadership as consistent with feminine virtue.

In the past, we've imagined that ancient women's lives were shaped by very restrictive ideals—basically, they should do whatever their father or husband told them to do and stay in the house. If you think of that as the cultural expectation for women, then any evidence of agency or action by women would seem to contradict these norms.

But ancient people didn't see these things as contradictory! In the previous chapter we saw that a woman honored as a patron or priest might also be praised for modesty. Another reason that virtue and leadership weren't contradictory was that there was more than one way to embody the role of a "good woman." Although the classic image was someone working at home, women's work on behalf of their families often took them far afield.

There was more than one way to embody the role of a "good woman."

And their labor was valued. So instead of seeming to oppose feminine virtues, industrious labor was another trait of a virtuous woman.

99

Hardworking Women

One of the classic feminine virtues was industry. Murdia's funeral inscription, which we encountered in the previous chapter, mentions industry along with other traditional virtues: "in modesty, propriety, chastity, obedience, wool-working, industry, and loyalty she was on an equal level with other good women." Women were honored for the work they did to keep their families going.

A kind of shorthand that developed for this was to say that a woman was devoted to her wool-working. You see that "wool-working" appears right next to "industry" among Murdia's virtues. In the previous chapter, we also looked at the burial inscription for Turia. Her husband honored her "tireless attention to wool-working." Figure 3 shows a funeral urn in the shape of a wool basket, to convey the deceased woman's devotion to her work.

Figure 3. Marble funeral urn in the shape of a wool basket; the Metropolitan Museum of Art / Art Resource, NY

The inclusion of wool-working as a trait honoring women is a pattern in this period. Here's another example, from the funeral inscription of a woman named Amymone: "Here lies Amymone, wife of Marcus, best and most beautiful, a worker in wool, pious, chaste, thrifty, faithful, devoted to their home."[1] Saying a woman was "a worker in wool" was a way to honor her as someone who fulfilled the traditional virtue of working hard for her family.

Why does wool-working show up in all these inscriptions? Why is it a placeholder for other activities? It may help to remember how difficult it is to make clothing. When I was growing up, my mom sewed a lot of my clothes, and that was labor-intensive—but she didn't actually make the fabric too! But for ancient people (and many people since that time), making clothes involved many steps: tending sheep and shearing sheep, washing and carding the wool, spinning, weaving, possibly dying the fabric, and then finally making clothes from it. And while men were sometimes involved in these steps (in the New Testament times, especially as weavers), the whole process was thought of as something women either did themselves or supervised.

In the New Testament period, it was no longer necessary for every woman to be engaged in wool-working. In the cities, it was actually possible to buy fabric. So it's interesting that the idea of wool-working persisted as a way to praise a woman who worked hard on behalf of her family. Even elite women, whom you *know* did not do much actual wool-working, were praised for making clothing for their families. Honoring a woman as a wool-worker did not mean she literally spent a lot of time spinning: it just meant she worked hard in ways that benefited the household.

As we talked about in chapter 4, women were involved in more occupations than we often imagine. They were doctors and midwives, teachers and administrators, musicians and athletes. Women owned and managed restaurants and many other kinds of businesses. They ran farms. While men also did these tasks, and usually got the more prestigious or lucrative jobs, we shouldn't imagine that women's work was restricted to sweeping floors and making meals or clothing. Their work took them into many arenas. And their labor on behalf of their families was regarded as virtuous.

A woman who did any of these jobs might have been praised as "a worker in wool." The important thing wasn't the specific job she had, but its larger purpose. A burial inscription like the one to Amymone doesn't actually tell us what she did for a living—it really just tells us that her family wanted to honor her and proclaim that she was a good person. To do so, they claimed that she fulfilled the feminine ideals. That lets us know that the ideals were still important. But the specific ways that she embodied them are lost to us. Women's industry took many forms. A woman who contributed her labor to benefit her household in any of these occupations might be honored as a "wool-worker."

Praising a wealthier woman like Turia or Murdia for wool-working was also a way of saying she was a virtuous woman devoted to her family. Her work included a variety of tasks other than carding wool, spinning, or weaving. Turia was quite wealthy, for example, and she would have likely spent less time actually making clothing and more time overseeing other people's labor. But her husband could still praise her for "tireless attention to wool-working."

One of the reasons why we modern people have seen women's virtue and action as contradictory is that we imagine a single ideal that shaped women's behavior. A woman just stays home and does housework, right? But in reality—just as in our culture today—there wasn't only one way to be acceptably feminine. Sure, people valued women as devoted to their families—like Amymone, who is honored for being "devoted to her home." But the same people valued women's industry. And they didn't see it as contradictory, even if her work took a woman outside of her house on a daily basis. There was more than one way to inhabit the role of the virtuous woman.

An example from our own culture might be helpful as a parallel. One piece of standard advice for building strong family bonds has been for parents and kids to eat dinner together. But even in families that eat dinner together frequently, there may often be nights when they don't eat together. When that happens, it's not because they've rejected the value that they feel strongly about on other nights! Instead, other priorities intervene—like the virtue of parents being diligent in their jobs, or the value of offering children a variety of (say, after-school) opportunities. From inside the culture, we don't experience these values as contradictory—as if we could only do one or the other. But in the moment, we do sometimes have to choose between them.

Ancient people hadn't given up on wool-working as an ideal. That's why they kept attributing it to women even when fewer women engaged in that work. But the virtue was still important to them, and they held onto it.

Ancient people hadn't given up on modesty, either, and exchanged it for the value of hard work. They continued to value both modesty and industry. So even though it might seem as if modesty would prevent women from making business deals or acting as a patron or running a shop, it didn't really work that way because modesty wasn't the only value people shared. They also valued hard work. (And, as we'll see in the next chapter, they also praised loyal action for the sake of one's family or city.) Women's work wasn't viewed as immodest. It was just one part of what it meant to live up to social expectations.

To summarize: modesty was an ideal virtue for women in this period. But we should not imagine the feminine virtues as social forces that only placed limitations on a woman's ability to act. Women who advocated for their communities or families were often affirmed as virtuous. These cases can appear paradoxical to modern interpreters because we assume a narrow definition of female virtue as subservience. But the attribution of modesty to active women points to a more complex set of values.

Active women were not countercultural renegades but were doing things that were socially acceptable.

We might think that a woman who was modest never left her home, or always did what the men around her told her to do. However, an industrious woman would need to be very busy working hard on behalf of her family. This work might take her outside of her home, and it might require that she give orders to others about the way that work should be done. She might undertake political advocacy on behalf of her family or seek out a new patron who could help the family's business run more smoothly. All of this would be virtuous action, and because of this it wouldn't be seen as contradicting the convention of feminine modesty. She wasn't necessarily viewed as an equal to all of the men around her, but the social norms still supported this kind of activity.

The interaction between the virtues also created a cultural climate in which being virtuous took on different forms. Instead of being confined to a single mold of feminine virtue, women pursued a variety of virtues under the particular circumstances their lives offered. This complexity also helps to explain why there is not a single role for women, defined by passivity and submission to men. The virtues supported a wider range of roles. The interaction of the virtues also suggests that active women were not countercultural renegades but were doing things that were socially acceptable.

The ability to see a wider set of possibilities for women's actions in antiquity is an important tool as we interpret evidence for women's economic and social roles and status. Communities could perceive active women as virtuous and not see them as doing something forbidden to women. The social norms of the time supported action and leadership by women as well as submissive behavior.

Industry in the New Testament

As we saw in chapter 4, the New Testament mentions only a few of the occupations of its women characters. Acts records Lydia's occupation as a "dealer in purple cloth" (Acts 16:14). The details of Lydia's business are not described there, but presumably this work supported her household and allowed her to offer hospitality to a visiting teacher like Paul. Additionally, both Prisca and Aquila are described as tentmakers (Acts 18:3). Again, few details are provided. Against the cultural background of the time, readers might well imagine that Prisca and Aquila worked together in their business as they traveled from place to place, and that Prisca contributed as much to the household economy as she did to the spread of the gospel.

Explore the virtue of industry in these passages:

ACTS 9:36–40

> In Joppa there was a disciple named Tabitha (in Greek her name is Dorcas); she was always doing good and helping the poor. About that time she became ill and died, and her body was washed and placed in an upstairs room. Lydda was near Joppa; so when the disciples heard that Peter was in Lydda, they sent two men to him

and urged him, "Please come at once!" Peter went with them, and when he arrived he was taken upstairs to the room. All the widows stood round him, crying and showing him the robes and other clothing that Dorcas had made while she was still with them. Peter sent them all out of the room; then he got down on his knees and prayed. Turning toward the dead woman, he said, "Tabitha, get up." She opened her eyes, and seeing Peter she sat up.

1. What wording points to women's labor?

2. What suggests that this activity is praiseworthy?

1 TIMOTHY 5:9–10

No widow may be put on the list of widows unless she is over sixty, has been faithful to her husband, and is well known for her good deeds, such as bringing up children, showing hospitality, washing the feet of the Lord's people, helping those in trouble and devoting herself to all kinds of good deeds.

1. What wording points to women's labor?

2. What suggests that this activity is praiseworthy?

10

Loyalty

Phoebe traveled to Rome and served as a patron and deacon, and yet she was also considered "commendable." In the past few chapters we've been considering how it was possible for someone like Phoebe to do all these things and still conform to traditional standards of femininity. We have a sense that women were expected to be passive and submissive. So, was an active woman like Phoebe a renegade? Or did social norms support this kind of behavior by women?

One way to answer this dilemma is via the classic virtue of loyalty. The burial inscriptions that we've already seen emphasize the importance of this virtue. In chapter 8 we met Murdia, whose son erected a funeral marker praising her. He wrote, "My dearest mother deserved greater praise than all others, since in modesty, propriety, chastity, obedience, wool-working, industry, and loyalty she was on an equal level with other good women, nor did she take second place to any woman in virtue, work and wisdom in times of danger."[1] Among the other attributes we've seen, Murdia's son highlights her loyalty.

Loyalty was action taken out of devotion to one's family, one's city, or the gods.

From our perspective, it may seem as if the expectation that a woman should be loyal to her family would mean that she couldn't think for herself or act independently. What we'll see in this chapter is that people of the time thought of loyalty as action taken out of devotion to one's family, one's city, or the gods.

Women Devoted to Their Families

Some examples of loyalty may fit our preconceptions. Listed alongside other classic virtues, loyalty might sound like passive acceptance of a husband's demands. When "loyalty" is listed at the end of a long list that also includes "propriety, chastity, and obedience," it's easy to think that loyalty narrowly means subservience.

Loyalty is also typically bundled together with other virtues like industry in the iconic attribute of wool-working. Wool-working, we remember, honored the labor that women performed for the benefit of their families. But this quality also conveys the idea that this hard work was undertaken for the benefit of the family, and so it also conveys her loyalty.

In fact, one of the most famous stories of wool-working, which would have been known to many early readers of the New Testament, was primarily an example of loyalty. In the *Odyssey*, Homer tells how Penelope waited faithfully for her husband, Odysseus, to return from the Trojan War. He was gone for years, and a lot of men approached Penelope saying that Odysseus must be dead, so she should marry them! But Penelope was loyal. At one point, she told the suitors they had to wait until she had finished weaving a burial shroud for her father-in-law, and then she would consider marriage. So, Penelope sat weaving this shroud every day, and at night she would unravel the work she had done. That way she didn't have to deal with all these marriage proposals! Penelope was an iconic woman of virtue, and her story combines the idea that wool-working was hard work with the sense that it is performed out of loyalty. It's a project for her father-in-law, and the way she goes about it shows her devotion to Odysseus.

When people mention a woman's wool-working, then, they are also indicating her loyalty to the family. This is the case with Turia, whom we first met in chapter 8. Her husband praised her "modesty, obedience, affability, and good nature" and her "tireless attention to wool-working."[2] He used words that let readers know of Turia's loyalty.

Examples of Loyalty

Like modesty, loyalty is a more complex virtue when you scratch the surface. It is more than just meeting your family's need for clothing! Let's consider some specific women who were praised for loyalty.

We've already mentioned Murdia, whose son lists her attributes, including loyalty. In the rest of the inscription, he praises her for a specific act of loyalty. You see, Murdia married, had children, and then her husband died. She inherited most of his property, some of which she kept for their children. Murdia later remarried. No one looked askance at that—it was expected, really. But a second marriage has the potential to complicate loyalty. Her son praised his mother as loyal because she had kept his father's property separate from the finances of her second marriage. In her will, she made sure that her first husband's property was passed on to his children. Her son makes it clear that Murdia had the authority to behave differently, but that by bequeathing her property this way she displayed her loyalty.

Loyalty is a more complex virtue when you scratch the surface.

Turia was another loyal woman whose actions might surprise us a bit today. The long inscription her husband wrote gives us many details about Turia's life, enabling us to see what led to this affirmation of her virtue. Her life was much more interesting than the initial list of virtues conveys. For one thing, her husband also praised her for avenging the deaths of her parents! And she provided financially for some of her female relatives. She was clearly a person with considerable property and initiative of her own.

In addition, the husband told this story about how Turia advocated successfully on his behalf. Turia and her husband lived through Rome's civil wars (just before the rise of Caesar Augustus, who was emperor when Jesus was born). Turia's husband was on the losing side of the war, but he had been pardoned by Caesar. But one of Caesar's close allies didn't acknowledge the pardon until Turia stepped in to insist. "When you threw yourself on the ground at his feet, not only did he not raise you up, but in fact he grabbed you and dragged you along as if you were a slave. You were covered with bruises, but with unflinching determination you reminded him of Augustus Caesar's edict of pardon."[3] Her husband praised Turia because she persisted through this hardship and helped to reestablish his own political standing!

Turia was praised for "modesty, obedience, affability, and good nature" *and also* for her successful defense of her husband during a time of national turmoil. These details in Turia's story are interesting because they present her as determined and actively pursuing her family's needs. And her husband doesn't seem to think there's any contradiction in the way he describes her. He doesn't say, "Oh, she was really modest most of the time, except when she confronted Lepidus," or "She was good-natured except when avenging her parents"! To him, the stories he tells *confirm* Turia's virtue.

The way Turia was honored may seem unusual to us, but similar praise occurs over and over in the sources of this period. Women were honored for perfecting traditional virtues at the same time that they undertook action on behalf of their families or communities. The actions women take are mentioned as evidence of their virtue, not as exceptions to it.

The actions women take are mentioned as evidence of their virtue.

Women like Turia and Murdia were praised because they actively pursued the needs of their families. Those needs included both political advocacy and management of property. At the same time, these women were also praised for modesty and obedience. In that historical context, these virtues had a broader range of meaning than we have often imagined.

Being a loyal woman involved the active pursuit of familial or communal needs. How did it make sense to people at the time that virtuous women could act in these ways? One important thing to understand is that there wasn't one single way that women could be commended for being virtuous. Today, it's common to assume that an ancient woman who was virtuous never spoke out or asserted her opinions forcefully. But in reality, people didn't value only submission; they valued other things as well.

One reason women's advocacy was acceptable was because it was interpreted as an act of loyalty. Turia's family was in a crisis, and she had enough social standing to assert her influence to try and change things for the better. The fact that she did so made life better for her family. So, that's good, right? A similar thing was true of Murdia. She distributed her late husband's property in her will to benefit the children they had together, and the fact that she did so was perceived as an expression of loyalty to her husband.

Loyalty to the family was really important, and it was related to the virtue of loyalty to the city and its gods. Allegiance to one's family was important for the way the family functioned and for the emotional bonds of its members. But loyalty to one's city or people also helped motivate patronage to the city. In the same way that people might work hard and sacrifice for their families, they might do the same for the city. All of this was seen as pleasing to the gods, who likewise demanded loyalty from the people they protected and aided.

Devotion to all three—gods, city, and family—was intertwined. When everything was going well, a person wouldn't have to choose between these entities. Working for your family meant protecting the interests of the city, and all of this was pleasing to the gods.

That's why women's loyalty to their families often overlaps with civic loyalty. Plutarch wrote a collection of stories about women who took brave action for the sake of their communities.

Women's loyalty to their families often overlaps with civic loyalty.

One story tells of a woman named Xenocrite, whose city was ruled by a tyrant, Aristodemus. Aristodemus had exiled her father and put her people to hard labor. Xenocrite pretended to like Aristodemus, and he was enamored with her. But she plotted with a few men who also opposed his rule. She gave them inside information to gain access to Aristodemus, and they overthrew him and restored democratic rule. Her people "chose her to be priestess of Demeter, feeling that the honor would be no less pleasing to the goddess than appropriate for Xenocrite."[4] Xenocrite showed loyalty both to her father and to her city, and her actions were seen as both courageous and pious.

But the interests of members of the family didn't always align with the good of the city! In cases where they became competing loyalties, devotion to one's god was considered the highest virtue, followed by allegiance to one's city, and only then came loyalty to family.

Plutarch recorded a number of sayings of women who declared their allegiance to their city even above their love for their families. For example, one woman "was burying her son, when a commonplace old woman came up to her and said 'Ah, the bad luck of it, you poor woman.' 'No, by heaven,' she said, 'but good luck; for I bore him that he might die for Sparta, and this is the very thing that has come to pass for me.'" This woman conveyed the notion that the well-being of the city was more important even than her own family members.

Plutarch also relates a situation in which the interests of family and city weren't aligned. He tells a story about a woman known only as the wife of Pythes. Her husband was the leader of their city, but he wasn't a very good one! He made his subjects work so hard in the gold mines that they couldn't do anything else, including grow enough food to feed themselves. The women of the town appealed to Pythes's wife, and she came up with a plan. When Pythes sat down for dinner one night, she presented him with a plate full of food that was made of gold. At first he thought it was cute, but when he realized that was all there was for dinner, he became upset. His wife said to him, "You're the one who has created an abundance of these things and nothing else. All other expertise and skills have vanished, and no one farms."[5] Because of her intervention, Pythes changed his mind and let most of the people go back to farming and other work.

If women were only supposed to be loyal and subservient to their husbands, you might think Plutarch would criticize Pythes's wife instead of praising her. But she displays her loyalty to the whole people, not just her immediate family. Now, ideally a woman's loyalty to her husband and family wouldn't be in conflict—because her husband wouldn't make such dumb decisions! Since Pythes's actions were harmful, she still showed virtue in her devotion to the people of the city. She used her influence to make policy changes for everyone's benefit.

In short, we shouldn't think of women's virtue as something that demanded subservience to men in every instance, or that required women to be passive while men led. There were lots of reasons why women acted of their own volition, and it wasn't wrong to do so. They were praised as virtuous when their actions expressed loyalty to their families and cities.

New Testament Loyalty

At first, it may seem as if the New Testament doesn't share the value of family loyalty with the culture at large. After all, Jesus tells one disciple not to return to bury his father (Matt. 8:21–22; Luke 9:59–60). But the idea here is that loyalty to God is higher than the obligation to family. If your familial loyalty conflicts with following Jesus, you should choose him over your family. This is similar to the view within the culture at large that devotion to the gods is the highest virtue.

We find another reframing of familial loyalty in Mark 3:34–35. Jesus rebuffs a visit from his mother and brothers, who are calling for him. Instead, "he looked at those seated in a circle around him and said, 'Here are my mother and my brothers! Whoever does God's will is my brother and sister and mother.'" In this case, Jesus creates a new set of family bonds for those who follow him. Loyalty to family still seems an important value, but the allegiance shifts to this new family. Again, the story reiterates that allegiance to God is a higher good than loyalty to one's family of origin.

But we also see some more conventional instances of family loyalty in the New Testament. In one example, the mother of the sons of

Zebedee approaches Jesus to ask him to give her sons a great reward. Kneeling before Jesus with her sons, she says, "Grant that one of these two sons of mine may sit at your right and the other at your left in your kingdom" (Matt. 20:21). In this case, we see a woman sticking her neck out to try and achieve something good for her children. Her request comes across as the wrong thing to ask for: Jesus says the position is not his to give, and then tells the disciples that the greatest among them is the servant (Matt. 20:23, 26–27). Nevertheless, early readers of this story would understand that what the mother was doing wasn't a bad thing. She was acting as an advocate for her sons.

Now explore the idea of loyalty in these passages.

THE CANAANITE WOMAN

A Canaanite woman from that vicinity came to him, crying out, "Lord, Son of David, have mercy on me! My daughter is demon-possessed and suffering terribly." Jesus did not answer a word. So his disciples came to him and urged him, "Send her away, for she keeps crying out after us." He answered, "I was sent only to the lost sheep of Israel." The woman came and knelt before him. "Lord, help me!" she said. He replied, "It is not right to take the children's bread and toss it to the dogs." "Yes it is, Lord," she said. "Even the dogs eat the crumbs that fall from their master's table." Then Jesus said to her, "Woman, you have great faith! Your request is granted." And her daughter was healed at that moment. (Matt. 15:22–28)

1. What does the woman do that conveys loyalty?

2. To whom is she loyal?

WOMEN AT JESUS'S DEATH, BURIAL, AND RESURRECTION

Matthew describes the presence of women at Jesus's death, burial, and resurrection this way:

> At the crucifixion: "Many women were there, watching from a distance. They had followed Jesus from Galilee to care for his needs. Among them were Mary Magdalene, Mary the mother of James and Joseph, and the mother of Zebedee's sons" (Matt. 27:55–56).

> At the burial: "Mary Magdalene and the other Mary were sitting there opposite the tomb" (Matt. 27:61).

> Easter Sunday: "After the Sabbath, at dawn on the first day of the week, Mary Magdalene and the other Mary went to look at the tomb" (Matt. 28:1).

1. What do the women do that conveys loyalty?

2. To whom are they loyal?

"OUR SISTER PHOEBE"

Paul introduces Phoebe as "our sister Phoebe" (Rom. 16:1). What does the familial language imply about the relationship between Phoebe, Paul, and the Roman church?

Marital Harmony

Let's imagine for a moment that Phoebe was married. If so, she seems to have been traveling without her husband to Rome. (She is introduced without mention of a husband.) Why is *she* credited as a patron, and not her husband? Was it possible for married women to act as Phoebe did without breaking the social conventions of marriage?

Interpreters of the Bible often imagine that the actions of married women were sharply restricted because women were subject to their husbands. We have frequently understood marriage as something that gave men complete dominance over their wives. So we have concluded that married women were subordinate to men—but also that virgins or widowed women might be free from these limitations. Some interpreters might conclude that Phoebe was unmarried because she plays an important role in the church yet her husband is not mentioned.

While there are social norms that state an ideal in which husbands were in charge, we have already seen a number of cultural practices that modify this picture. Wives owned and managed their own property. Even the dowry, which the husband controlled during the marriage, technically belonged to the wife and was eventually returned to her. We have also seen wives being honored for their civic leadership.

How do these things fit together? In this chapter, we'll continue to think about how ancient people understood and applied the rules of culture surrounding marital relationships. The ancients always assumed that it was better when husbands took the lead. But that preference didn't restrict women's abilities in the ways we have thought. If a marriage was working smoothly, both husband and wife would actively pursue the good of their family, using the influence and resources they had.

Both husband and wife would actively pursue the good of their family.

The Ideal of Marital Harmony

It's true that the ideal was for husbands to be in charge. Remember that husbands were usually five to ten years older than the women they married. They had higher status because of their age, and they also had more life experience, and probably more education. Because these social resources gave them an advantage, it made sense to people of the time that their young brides would defer to them.

The philosopher Plutarch wrote an entire treatise on marriage, in which he presents the model situation as one in which the husband has higher status than the wife and she yields to him. At one point, he compares the husband and wife to a king and a philosopher. The king, who has higher status, can gain honor by being a patron of philosophy—that's the right way to go about it. However, if the philosopher tries too hard to win the king's favor, he probably ends up diminishing his own reputation—and perhaps the king's too. Like philosophers, wives have lower standing. Women who submit to their husbands acknowledge the social distinction of husbands' greater status.

In the same paragraph, Plutarch gives a picture of what the husband's "rule" over the wife should be like. He writes, "But the husband should rule the wife, not as a master rules a slave, but as the soul rules the body, sharing her feelings and growing together with her in affection. That is the just way. One can care for one's body without being a slave to its pleasures and desires; and one can rule a wife while giving her enjoyment and kindness."[1]

Here, Plutarch specifies the ideal relationship. The husband is in charge, but never in a violent way. People were allowed to use corporal punishment with those they enslaved, but not with free people, and the husband should not treat his wife like a slave. The gold standard was the wise husband, who could lead his household without the use of force.

Situations That Weren't Ideal

Of course, most marriages were not ideal, at least not all the time! So we shouldn't imagine that Plutarch's words were consistently applied, yielding happy marriages everywhere. In fact, Plutarch's treatise acknowledges many ways that marriages strayed from the ideal. From these stories and other evidence, we gain a sense of the options women had when things weren't ideal. These scenarios tell us something about the balance of power between husbands and wives in their relationships.

In an extreme situation, divorce was an option for husbands or wives to pursue. In chapter 3, we saw part of a court document for Tryphaine, who says her husband "squandered [the dowry], abused and insulted me, and, laying his hands on me, he used me as if I were his bought slave"[2]—just what Plutarch says not to do. As a result, she divorced her husband and petitioned the court to make him repay her dowry. Although there were social forces that encouraged people to stay married, they didn't have to, and women like Tryphaine could divorce their husbands and reclaim their dowries.

The dowry gave the husband incentive to work things out.

The fact that the husband had to return the dowry in the event of divorce gave women some power in their relationships with their husbands. Although dowries weren't typically a large proportion of a couple's wealth, you can imagine how some husbands would rather have the dowry than not. The dowry gave the husband some incentive to work things out with his spouse.

Some sources suggest that a rich wife would have more power in the relationship than her husband. This is not only because she could leave with her dowry; it was also because wealthy people simply had more social status. A rich wife created a "problem" for a mar-

A wealthy wife could have greater social standing than her husband.

riage because of the ideal that said husbands should be in charge. A woman with more wealth than her husband could overcome the social disparity created by his age, experience, and education, and end up the more power-ful one in the relationship. The male writers of the time disparaged such situations—one said you wouldn't want to be your "wife's wife," meaning that the husband of a rich wife would have less status and would therefore become the "wife." But in that remark, we see the author's assumption that the husband should have higher status and the reality that wives had some power. A wealthy wife could have greater social standing than her husband.

The social power wives had wasn't simply a bad thing either. Some men were glad to have a wife who was wealthier than they were. She would have a larger dowry and many important social connections that could make his own business dealings much more profitable. Women had both money and cultural capital and could use it on be-half of their families. Elite men might look down on the situation as less than ideal. But the people in those marriages could have been quite happy with the way things were.

Marital Harmony in Practice

It's no wonder, then, given the real social standing and wealth that women had in this period, that couples placed a premium on marital harmony. Since a husband and a wife both had some social influ-ence, they could work together to promote the interests of the whole household. But if they worked at odds with each other, or didn't see their interests as connected, then they could also make life more dif-ficult for one another.

The ideal of marital harmony is often stated explicitly in burial monuments. These inscriptions are meant to represent the best side of a relationship, so they don't give us the whole picture by any means. But they do tell us that couples *wanted* to depict their marriages as harmonious. These ideals show up over and over in memorials of the time.

But these inscriptions can also give us a glimpse of the lives that were possible for married women. For example, in chapter 4, we saw this funeral commemoration of a female doctor: "To Primilla, a physician, daughter of Lucius Vibius Melito. She lived 44 years, of which 30 she spent with Lucius Coecceius Apthorus without a quarrel. Apthorus built this monument for his best, chaste wife and for himself."[3] Primilla was a knowledgeable person with a medical practice. The inscription suggests a woman with social standing and the capacity for independent action, not one whose husband controlled every aspect of her life. Yet her husband also remembers the marriage as harmonious, "without a quarrel." To the extent that this was true, it reflects their ability to view their interests and goals as shared rather than separate.

The inscription honoring Turia is much longer and shows how a wife could use her power to achieve something for her family. As we saw in chapter 10, Turia's husband praised her as a paragon of feminine virtues, and he also hailed her advocacy on his behalf. She had substantial social influence, and she put it to work for the good of her entire family, advocating on behalf of her husband with a powerful politician. Turia's use of her social power on his behalf is an example of marital harmony.

Plutarch's treatise *Advice to the Bride and Groom* also suggests there was more give-and-take in ancient marriages. The husband should not antagonize his wife—for example, he should not come home smelling of another woman's perfume! And the wife should not hang out with women who always criticize her husband. So, even though Plutarch says the husband should "rule" the wife, he also advises that both parties modify their own behavior in order to achieve harmony.

Plutarch's treatise is addressed to a young woman named Eurydice on the occasion of her marriage. Eurydice was Plutarch's pupil, which means she was an advanced student who studied philosophy. And Eurydice's mother, Clea, was a friend of Plutarch's, and he dedicated to her another treatise he wrote. Later on in Eurydice's life, her daughter would commission a statue honoring Eurydice as a priestess of the shrine of Apollo at Delphi. So if Eurydice and her husband took Plutarch's advice and lived out the ideal, she still had the capacity to pursue civic responsibilities and to act as a patron.

Some social norms reinforced men's power over women, but the disparity wasn't so pronounced that women had no ability to act independently of their husbands. As we've seen, legal norms granted women authority over their property, and social benefits existed for families where women had social standing. I'm not suggesting that husbands and wives viewed each other as equals—that seems unlikely. But the ideal of marital harmony suggests that they valued the ability to balance their interests and work together. And they *needed* to work together because both had property and social resources at their disposal.

They valued the ability to balance their interests and work together.

Marital Harmony in the New Testament

For the most part, the relationship between husbands and wives doesn't show up in stories of the New Testament. We know that some of the disciples were married; Simon, at least, had a mother-in-law (Mark 1:30). But we never get to see them interacting with their spouses as a part of the narrative. Nevertheless, one story in Acts mentions a married couple and their property. Although it is not the woman's property at issue, it's an interesting story for what it conveys about marriage:

> Now a man named Ananias, together with his wife Sapphira, also sold a piece of property. With his wife's full knowledge he kept back part of the money for himself, but brought the rest and put it at the apostles' feet. Then Peter said, "Ananias, how is it that Satan has so filled your heart that you have lied to the Holy Spirit and have kept for yourself some of the money you received for the land? Didn't it belong to you before it was sold? And after it was sold, wasn't the money at your disposal? What made you think of doing such a thing? You have not lied just to human beings but to God." When Ananias heard this, he fell down and died. (Acts 5:1–5)

Sapphira subsequently lies to the apostles as well, and she dies also (Acts 5:7–10).

Of the many interesting things in this story, let's focus on the relationship between the married couple. This property belongs to Ananias: as Peter says, "Didn't it belong to you before it was sold?" But the story says that Ananias and his wife agree *together* to sell the property. When Peter accuses Sapphira, he says, "How could you *conspire* to test the Spirit of the Lord?" (5:9). So here we have a married couple making decisions together about the man's property. They also agree to deceive the group about the wealth they own.

Although Ananias and Sapphira are clearly a negative example because of their dishonesty, readers of this story are not meant to be surprised that the husband and wife acted in concert regarding the management of their property. In fact, the death of Sapphira would surely appear unjust if she was not really a partner in decision making with her husband. By law, Ananias did not have to consult Sapphira in order to sell his property. But by social custom, a good marriage involved consideration of the couple's joint interests. The story presents Sapphira as entering willingly into her husband's deception and thus as deserving punishment.

Their families often needed and wanted women to have and use power.

In other parts of the New Testament, we see affirmations of the culture's ideal, which stated that wives should defer to husbands and husbands should love their wives and treat them well. When we read these passages in the New Testament without the cultural background in mind, we can forget the social supports for women's independent action—and the fact that their families often needed and wanted women to have and use power. The New Testament language comes across as more restrictive than what seems likely to have been actual practice.

Below, we'll consider two passages that convey standards of household harmony and then imagine how some New Testament couples might have understood their own relationships to embody this ideal.

ONE STANDARD OF HOUSEHOLD HARMONY

This long passage from Ephesians is the version of this teaching most often cited today.

> Submit to one another out of reverence for Christ. Wives, submit yourselves to your own husbands as you do to the Lord. For the husband is the head of the wife as Christ is the head of the church, his body, of which he is the Savior. Now as the church submits to Christ, so also wives should submit to their husbands in everything. Husbands, love your wives, just as Christ loved the church and gave himself up for her to make her holy, cleansing her by the washing with water through the word, and to present her to himself as a radiant church, without stain or wrinkle or any other blemish, but holy and blameless. In this same way, husbands ought to love their wives as their own bodies. He who loves his wife loves himself. After all, no one ever hated their own body, but they feed and care for their body, just as Christ does the church—for we are members of his body. "For this reason a man will leave his father and mother and

be united to his wife, and the two will become one flesh." This is a profound mystery—but I am talking about Christ and the church. However, each one of you also must love his wife as he loves himself, and the wife must respect her husband. (Eph. 5:21–33)

1. Ephesians differs from Plutarch's teaching in its Christian theology. However, there are a number of similarities between the two. Here's the quotation from Plutarch for comparison:

If wives submit to their husbands, they are praised. If they try to rule them, they cut a worse figure than their subjects. But the husband should rule the wife, not as a master rules a slave, but as the soul rules the body, sharing her feelings and growing together with her in affection. That is the just way. One can care for one's body without being a slave to its pleasures and desires; and one can rule a wife while giving her enjoyment and kindness.[4]

List the language that you think is relevant from each quotation in the category listed.

	Plutarch	Ephesians
Wives should . . .		
Husbands should . . .		

Describe how both authors compare the wife to the husband's body.

2.   Consider Priscilla and Aquila, a couple who worked as evangelists (and tentmakers) with Paul. In Acts, we hear this about them:

> Meanwhile a Jew named Apollos, a native of Alexandria, came to Ephesus. He was a learned man, with a thorough knowledge of the Scriptures. He had been instructed in the way of the Lord, and he spoke with great fervor and taught about Jesus accurately, though he knew only the baptism of John. He began to speak boldly in the synagogue. When Priscilla and Aquila heard him, they invited him to their home and explained to him the way of God more adequately. (Acts 18:24-26)

In Romans, Paul also addresses Priscilla and Aquila, who have returned to Rome: "Greet Priscilla and Aquila, my co-workers in Christ Jesus. They risked their lives for me. Not only I but all the churches of the Gentiles are grateful to them" (Rom. 16:3-4).

Imagine that Priscilla died and Aquila was writing her burial inscription. What would he say? In particular, does Aquila think Priscilla has fulfilled the Christian ideal as stated in Ephesians 5:21-32, or has she done something different? State reasons for your answer.

ANOTHER VERSION OF THE SAME IDEAL

Colossians also has a shorter statement of the same ideal:

> Wives, submit yourselves to your husbands, as is fitting in the Lord. Husbands, love your wives and do not be harsh with them. (Col. 3:18-19)

Of the women patrons Luke mentions, only one is explicitly said to be married:

> Jesus traveled about from one town and village to another, proclaiming the good news of the kingdom of God. The Twelve were with him, and also some women who had been cured of evil spirits and diseases: Mary (called Magdalene) from whom seven demons had come out; Joanna the wife of Chuza, the manager of Herod's household; Susanna; and many others. These women were helping to support them out of their own means. (Luke 8:1–3)

Imagine that Joanna's husband is commemorating her after her death. Would he say their marriage fulfilled the ideal of Colossians 3:18–19?

PART 4

Speech and Silence

Everyday Speech

Did Phoebe speak to the church in Rome? Paul's letter doesn't give us that information. Many scholars conclude that Phoebe likely did read Paul's letter aloud to the Roman congregation, based on cultural practices of the time. In chapter 7 we discussed whether it was likely that Phoebe was able to read the letter. But even if Phoebe knew how to read, that still doesn't tell us whether it would have been acceptable for her to read in front of a group of people. So in these next chapters we consider patterns of women's speech during this period.

Modern readers are often familiar with the ideal of women's silence in the ancient world. Women could be criticized for talking too much or for speaking in front of men to whom they should defer. The culture prized excellent and persuasive speech, but these skills were expected only of men of high standing. In the abstract, women were indeed idealized as deferring to men in their speech.

But in light of the previous chapters, it may not be surprising to find that ancient evidence also shows women speaking. Indeed, the kind of social and economic interactions I have described so far often required speech. In some cases, women's social interactions entailed speaking, whether they were seeking out a patron's help or responding to someone who wanted their assistance. Similarly, owning and managing property involved giving instructions

Ancient evidence shows women speaking.

or making sales and purchases, all of which involved speech. Women's occupations often required speaking as well. As in the other arenas we have considered, there is considerable evidence that women's speech was a normal and expected part of life. Gendered inequalities affected women's lives, but they were not the whole story.

This chapter explores *everyday* circumstances that would have required women speaking—in civic, social, and business contexts, to men as well as women. In chapter 13, we'll examine speech that is specifically religious in nature. And then in chapters 14 and 15, we'll look again at the ideal of silence to understand how it fits with this evidence.

Business and Social Contexts

Women spoke in many contexts in the course of their daily lives. They completed business transactions and gave instructions to others. Consider this carving from a marketplace in Ostia, Rome's port city (fig. 4). A female proprietor is depicted selling her wares. As we saw in chapter 4, such occupations were common for women. In another inscription from Rome, a husband commemorated his wife, Abudia Megiste, following her death. He praised her as "most loyal" and stated her occupation: "she was a seller of fruit and legumes at the central steps."[1] Like others who sold products at market, these women spoke as they communicated with buyers and made deals.

Such markets were often thriving businesses. In each of these cases, it's likely the woman ran a busy enterprise. These were not vegetable stands in remote locations. Ostia, the city where the above image was found, was Rome's port city, so it was an important location for trade. And Abudia's husband identifies her location in Rome as well, "at the central steps." We can imagine these women as proprietors of successful businesses. Their speech was expected as a matter of course.

Another occupation that involved a lot of speaking was teaching. Women who were teachers spoke to the children they taught, of

Figure 4. *Funerary stele relief of a vegetable and poultry shop; Erich Lessing /*
Art Resource, NY

course. But they also addressed parents and those who accompanied
the children to school.

Furthermore, women engaged in social activities that involved
speaking. Women and men attended dinner parties together in this
period. The satirist Juvenal criticized the fashions of his day, both for
men and for women. In one passage he laments the woman who, as
soon as she sits down to dinner, is praising poets and comparing them
to each other. "The schoolteachers give way, the teachers of rhetoric
are beaten, the whole party falls silent, there'll not be a word from
any lawyer or auctioneer—and not even from another woman. Such
vigorous verbiage pours from her, you'd say it was the sound of people
bashing all their bowls and bells at once."[2] Juvenal's criticism clearly
implies that women should not speak so much. But the picture he
paints was also meant to be familiar to his readers, and it suggests a
context in which women's speech was common.

Letters also suggest how women spoke as a part of their daily business. While not exactly the same thing as speech, letters give us a
glimpse of how a woman might have interacted if she were there in

person. Consider this letter from Apollonous (a woman) to Julius
Terentianus, who is probably her husband. Terentianus was a soldier,
and Apollonous is managing their business and writing to him about
it: "And about your fields, I have reduced your brother's rent to the
extent of two artabai. Now I receive from him eight artabai of wheat
and six artabai of vegetable seed. And do not worry about us and take
care of yourself."[3] Apollonous's letter gives us a glimpse of what her
spoken communication might have been like. It also identifies tasks
that entailed her speaking to others to arrange these matters.

Here is another letter from a woman to her mother: "Taorsenouphis to Ision her mother, many greetings. . . . Please give your
share of the crop from the vineyard to my sister,
and a bunch of grapes. I sent you three pairs of
bowls, one for you and one for Petesouchos and
one for the sons-in-law of your sister, and a little
cup for little Theonas, and another for the daughter of your sister. And
if you receive lentils, send them to me by Katoitos."[4]

She gives instructions she
expects will be followed.

In both of these letters, we see the basic, everyday interactions that
were necessary for many people. They involve the exchange of goods,
including valuable property like vineyards. The tone of the second
letter suggests that the woman understands herself as the manager of
these items, and she gives instructions she expects will be followed.
We can imagine that, if she were present in person, she would speak
in the same manner.

Advocacy

In addition to business interests, women also spoke to advocate
for their political and social needs. Most of the time, there was no
record that they did so, and these moments are lost to us historically. However, a number of authors recorded important historical
interventions by women. Often, the stories involved women of high
standing who were in a position to influence the men around them.

But it seems likely that lower-class women also spoke to advocate for their needs, and did so in ways that were appropriate for their social position. These women spoke boldly to influence the course of events and were praised when the outcome benefited the whole community. One example of an upper-class woman that we've already seen is Turia (see chapter 9), whose husband recounted how she approached a high-ranking politician and pleaded on her spouse's behalf. Although she encountered resistance, her efforts were successful in the end.

Another example comes from Plutarch's story of Chilonis, whose husband and father were fighting to be king of Sparta. Her husband's side was defeated, and the question then was what would happen to him. Before a large gathering, Chilonis appealed to her father not to kill her husband but to exile him instead. She spoke eloquently about her personal sorrow, but also the importance of the decision for the whole city. She argued that killing her husband would be the act of a tyrant rather than a wise ruler. Her speech persuaded her father, who sent her husband into exile.

There are numerous other examples of such political speech by women. One narrative from a Jewish context is Judith's story, which begins with a long narration of the political turmoil in her town. Holofernes and his troops had besieged the Israelites, and the leaders of the town agreed to surrender to him in five days. When Judith learned of this,

> She sent her maid . . . to summon Chabris and Charmis, the elders of her town. They came to her, and she said to them: "Listen to me, rulers of the people of Bethulia! What you have said to the people today is not right; you have even sworn and pronounced this oath between God and you, promising to surrender the town to our enemies unless the Lord turns and helps us within so many days. Who are you to put God to the test today, and to set yourselves up in the place of God in human affairs?" (Jth. 8:10–12)

It may seem surprising to find a woman dressing down the leaders of her town in this way. But ancient readers would not have found this problematic. Indeed, bold speech on behalf of one's city or family was often seen as virtuous. In the examples provided, the women addressed situations that affected the safety and well-being of their whole city. Their speech was judged wise and virtuous. Their willingness to speak out at a time of civic crisis was evidence of their devotion to the good of their community.

In another case, the Roman historian Livy tells the story of women rallying in the streets to persuade senators to repeal laws that restricted displays of wealth. The laws had been enacted in a time of war so that riches could be used for military spending. But later, in *Bold speech on* a more peaceful and prosperous time, people wanted to *behalf of one's city or* be able to display their status through their clothing and *family was often seen* jewelry. The women protested in the streets around the *as virtuous.* Forum, where the Roman Senate met. Senators made arguments both for and against the repeal, but in the end the women's protest was successful and the laws were repealed.[5]

To understand the social rules around women's speech, we need to take evidence like this into account. Women's speech was sometimes criticized. But women also conducted their business, maintained social relationships, and advocated for their interests. Indeed, they were sometimes praised for doing so.

Everyday Speech in the New Testament

Alongside ideals about women's silence, we find evidence that women's speech was an expected and necessary part of their everyday lives. Some women engaged in speech with political overtones. Many women spoke in the course of their daily activities as they pursued the economic and social needs of their families.

The stories of the New Testament reflect the social conventions to which first-century readers were accustomed. In the passage about the

Canaanite woman (Matt. 15:21–28; cf. Mark 7:24–30), a mother seeks Jesus's help to heal her daughter from an illness. Although she encounters resistance, she continues to make her request known, and in the end, Jesus heals her daughter. In John 11, Mary and Martha send a message to Jesus requesting similar help for their brother (John 11:3).

The mother of the sons of Zebedee advocates for her family in a different way when she asks Jesus if her sons can sit at Jesus's right and left side in his kingdom (Matt. 20:20–28). Although she may misunderstand the nature of Jesus's kingdom to some extent, her request of assistance for her sons would have been comprehensible at that time.

Priscilla is a woman who teaches about Christ, although she is not quoted directly in this narrative. Priscilla, or Prisca as she is also called, has some prominence in the New Testament because she is mentioned repeatedly. Paul greets her in the closing of Romans, "Greet Priscilla and Aquila, my co-workers in Christ Jesus" (Rom. 16:3; cf. 2 Tim. 4:19). Although Paul had not yet been to Rome, he knew Priscilla and her husband from his travels. According to Acts, Paul met them in Corinth, and

Women's speech was an expected and necessary part of their everyday lives.

because they were all tentmakers by trade, he stayed with them while he proclaimed the gospel there (Acts 18:1–2). The couple accompanied Paul to Ephesus, where they parted ways. Priscilla and Aquila then met a man named Apollos, who knew the baptism of John but not of the Holy Spirit. "[Apollos] began to speak boldly in the synagogue. When Priscilla and Aquila heard him, they invited him to their home and explained to him the way of God more adequately" (Acts 18:26). Most of these texts name Priscilla first, which suggests that she was more prominent than her husband. (Otherwise, the common practice would have been to mention him first.) They teach together in this passage, as they may also have done in "the church that meets at their house" (1 Cor. 16:19).

Also often overlooked is the story in which Peter is accused of being one of Jesus's disciples. In all four Gospels, Peter is questioned and denies his association with Jesus. And in each case, the first person to question Peter is a woman. Mark writes, "While Peter was below in the courtyard, one of the servant girls of the high priest came by. When she saw Peter warming himself, she looked closely at him. 'You also were with that Nazarene, Jesus,' she said. But he denied it. 'I don't know or understand what you're talking about,' he said, and went out into the entryway" (Mark 14:66–68). This girl is not an elite person, although her position with the high priest would have given her some social standing. She recognizes Peter as an associate of the accused man, Jesus, and she speaks about it openly. Her words prompt Peter's first denial of Jesus.

Herodias is one of the most elite women to speak in the Gospels, and her speech is also political in nature. Prompted by Herod to name any gift, she asks for the head of John the Baptist (Mark 6:24), and Herod has John executed to fulfill her wish. This was a conventional type of story in the New Testament period: a ruler at a dinner party exhibits little self-control, and the result is an injustice. The idea that women had political desires and access to power, even in this round-about way, is also assumed to be common knowledge.

Now explore the speech of women in these passages.

THE WIDOW AND THE UNJUST JUDGE

Then Jesus told his disciples a parable to show them that they should always pray and not give up. He said, "In a certain town there was a judge who neither feared God nor cared what people thought. And there was a widow in that town who kept coming to him with the plea, 'Grant me justice against my adversary.' For some time he refused. But finally he said to himself, 'Even though I don't fear God or care what people think, yet because this widow keeps bothering me, I will see that she gets justice, so that she won't eventually come and attack me!'" (Luke 18:1–5)

1. What does the woman say in the story?

2. How would you identify the nature of her speech (e.g., political, religious, personal)?

3. What result does her speech have?

PILATE'S WIFE

The way Matthew tells the story of Jesus's trial, Pilate prefers to release Jesus. One line in the story that is easy to overlook gives Pilate's wife a role in the story:

> While Pilate was sitting on the judge's seat, his wife sent him this message: "Don't have anything to do with that innocent man, for I have suffered a great deal today in a dream because of him." But the chief priests and the elders persuaded the crowd to ask for Barabbas and to have Jesus executed. (Matt. 27:19–20)

1. What does the woman say in the story?

2. How would you identify the nature of her speech (e.g., political, religious, personal)?

3. What result does her speech have?

LYDIA

> From Troas we put out to sea and sailed straight for Samothrace,
> and the next day we went on to Neapolis. From there we traveled
> to Philippi, a Roman colony and the leading city of that district of
> Macedonia. And we stayed there several days. On the Sabbath we
> went outside the city gate to the river, where we expected to find
> a place of prayer. We sat down and began to speak to the women
> who had gathered there. One of those listening was a woman from
> the city of Thyatira named Lydia, a dealer in purple cloth. She was a
> worshiper of God. The Lord opened her heart to respond to Paul's
> message. When she and the members of her household were bap-
> tized, she invited us to her home. "If you consider me a believer
> in the Lord," she said, "come and stay at my house." And she per-
> suaded us. (Acts 16:11–15)

1. What does the woman say in the story?

2. How would you identify the nature of her speech (e.g., political,
religious, personal)?

3. What result does her speech have?

13

Prayer and Prophecy

There were probably many situations in which Phoebe spoke. She completed her work (whatever it was). She was a deacon. And as a patron, she both received and responded to requests. All of these things get us closer to understanding the context in which Phoebe may have spoken to the Roman church.

But there's more we want to know. We also want to understand whether people of her day would have found it acceptable for women to speak in a church meeting. Did religious speech in particular, either in the church or in the culture at large, restrict women's participation?

This chapter addresses conventions of women's speech in *religious* contexts. Ancient narratives described women speaking in religious contexts without any indication that they were doing something wrong. There were many kinds of religious speech that were possible, and we don't have lots of evidence for many of them—either for men or for women. We'll stick to areas in which we have quite a bit of evidence: women's participation in prayer and in prophecy.

Prayer

Ancient prayers were usually voiced out loud, rather than silently, as is often the custom today. Prayer, then, was speech. There are many examples of women's prayer in ancient texts.

One example of a woman praying is from Judith. We saw in the previous chapter how Judith speaks to the elders of her town. Judith also prays for God's deliverance as she sets out to approach the surrounding enemy. It's a lengthy prayer that begins with Judith recounting the ways God's power has saved Israel in the past. Then she turns to the present:

> "Here now are the Assyrians, a greatly increased force, priding themselves in their horses and riders, boasting in the strength of their foot soldiers, and trusting in shield and spear, in bow and sling. They do not know that you are the Lord who crushes wars; the Lord is your name. Break their strength by your might, and bring down their power in your anger; for they intend to defile your sanctuary, and to pollute the tabernacle where your glorious name resides, and to break off the horns of your altar with the sword. Look at their pride, and send your wrath upon their heads. Give to me, a widow, the strong hand to do what I plan. By the deceit of my lips strike down the slave with the prince and the prince with his servant; crush their arrogance by the hand of a woman.
>
> "For your strength does not depend on numbers, nor your might on the powerful. But you are the God of the lowly, helper of the oppressed, upholder of the weak, protector of the forsaken, savior of those without hope. Please, please, God of my father, God of the heritage of Israel, Lord of heaven and earth, Creator of the waters, King of all your creation, hear my prayer!" (Jth. 9:7–12)

Here Judith acknowledges God's might and asks for God to save her people. She goes on in the story to trick the opposing military leader, Holofernes, and to behead him.

Judith's story is likely a fictional account. I do not mean to claim that we see the real speech of an ancient woman here. However, in reading fictional stories, we gain important historical information, because we see what ancient readers took for granted as conventional actions of men and women. Readers would not be surprised that Judith prays eloquently. Her brave action in the story is extraordinary, but nothing suggests that her speech is unusual.

Judith offered this prayer when she was by herself. However, it doesn't seem quite right to think of it as "private" prayer, for the narrator states that Judith prays "at the very time when the evening incense was being offered in the house of God in Jerusalem" (Jth. 9:1). By praying at this hour, Judith aligns her prayer with this moment of corporate religious significance. Furthermore, the subject of the prayer was not personal but political. Judith takes on the role in the narrative of one who intervenes with God on behalf of the people. Many similar examples of prayers are recorded in the stories of this time period.

Other prayers by women were offered in corporate settings. Third Maccabees, like Judith one of the apocryphal books of the Bible, tells the story of Jews living in Egypt and persecuted by the tyrant Ptolemy. Ptolemy devises a plan to gather the Jews together and attack them with elephants. Three times the Jews pray to God, who makes Ptolemy's plans go awry. The text states explicitly who is gathered the third time they pray: "Parents and children, mothers and daughters, and others with babies at their breasts who were drawing their last milk. . . . When they considered the help that they had received before from heaven, they prostrated themselves with one accord on the ground, removing the babies from their breasts, and cried out in a very loud voice, imploring the Ruler over every power to manifest himself and be merciful to them, as they stood now at the gates of death" (3 Macc. 5:49-51).

God responds to their prayers, sending two angels, who turn the elephants against the very army that had goaded them along. The prayer of the whole people brings this response of salvation. Ancient readers would not have been astonished by the prayers of women among this group.

Although these two examples come from Jewish sources, it was also conventional for women of all religious traditions to pray in temples and shrines. For example, in one Greek story a woman named Anthia is pursued by a powerful man, Polyidus, who wants to have sex with her. But Anthia loves another man named Habrocomes and wants to escape. She runs to the temple of Isis and takes refuge there. She prays to Isis, "Mistress of Egypt, who time and again have assisted me, please be my savior once more. Let Polyidus too spare me, as with your help I keep myself chaste for Habrocomes."[1] Polyidus reveres Isis as well, and he promises to leave Anthia alone. In other parts of the story, Anthia voices prayers at the temple of Apis in Memphis and at the temple of Helius in Rhodes.

Some of the evidence for women's prayers comes from inscriptions crafted to commemorate these moments. People would often write prayers to the gods, either on paper or on the temple walls. Sometimes people would offer something to the gods with a vow in hopes of having their prayer answered. Anthia's story records a similar situation. When she is in Rhodes at the temple of Helius, she cuts off her hair as an offering to the god and gives it with an inscription: "On behalf of her husband Habrocomes, Anthia dedicated her hair to the god."[2] This example

Women prayed in temples and homes and arenas.

of an inscription was recorded in a Greek novel, but many other actual inscriptions like this have been found by archaeologists. Both men and women made these donations. Cutting off one's hair as one made a vow or prayer to the gods was a type of votive offering that sometimes accompanied such prayers.

As we have seen in these examples, women prayed in temples and homes and arenas. Both women and men spoke these prayers, on their own behalf or on behalf of a group of people. Whatever the case, ancient writers present the prayers of women as a common occurrence.

Prophecy

Other evidence shows that women were prophets. If prayer was human speech to God, prophecy was communication that went the other way, from God to human beings. It was quite common for ancient people to seek insight from a deity about human events. And women were oracles or prophets of Jewish and other Greek and Roman deities.

For example, the shrine of Apollo at Delphi was a famous site at which women prophesied. People traveled long distances to seek an oracle at Delphi. Cities commissioned groups to do the same so that the city leaders could confirm their actions. Although Delphi was the most well-known site where women prophesied, at many other locations women conveyed the wishes of the gods.

Another famous group of prophets were the Sibyls. The Sibyls were usually older women, and their prophetic work spanned many centuries. There were Sibyls from all around the Mediterranean and beyond, including Jewish Sibyls (and later on, Christian ones). The Sibyls prophesied orally, but their *Women were prophets.* sayings were collected and written down, the most famous collection of which was located at Rome. It was consulted for official state purposes, authorized by a decree of the Senate. Over many centuries, the Sibyls were influential prophets.

Prayer and Prophecy in the New Testament

The New Testament conveys the convention of prayer and prophecy by women, both inside and outside the church. In Paul's letter to the church in Corinth, he takes for granted that women in that community prayed and prophesied. "Every man who prays or prophesies with his head covered dishonors his head. But every woman who prays or prophesies with her head uncovered dishonors her head—it is the same as having her head shaved" (1 Cor. 11:4–5). There are gendered differences in dress here, but no difference in the expectation that both women and men will pray and prophesy in church.

As he continues these instructions in 1 Corinthians 12–14, Paul emphasizes the importance of prophecy for the worshiping community. In ranking the spiritual gifts, he names prophets as second only to apostles (and ahead of teachers; 1 Cor. 12:28). And he encourages everyone to "eagerly desire the greater gifts" (12:31), especially prophecy (14:1, 39).

In the ancient church, prophecy was both common and important. Although prayer is a more familiar form of speech for us today, we should not overlook the importance of prophecy in Paul's experience and teaching. Women were some of those with prophetic gifts, and they were expected to speak for the group when they had a message from God.

Luke and Acts show a good deal of interest in prophecy, and we see explicit references to women who prophesy. The first is Anna, who encounters the infant Jesus in Luke 2:36–38. Luke writes, "There was also a prophet, Anna, the daughter of Phanuel, of the tribe of Asher. She was very old; she had lived with her husband seven years after her marriage, and then was a widow until she was eighty-four. She never left the temple but worshiped night and day, fasting and praying. Coming up at that very moment, she gave thanks to God and spoke about the child to all who were looking forward to the redemption of Jerusalem." Luke identifies Anna as a prophet, and she speaks openly in the temple about Jesus's identity.

Another example of women who prophesy is the four daughters of Philip. During his travels, Paul stays at their home. "Leaving the next day, we reached Caesarea and stayed at the house of Philip the evangelist, one of the Seven. He had four unmarried daughters who prophesied" (Acts 21:8–9). This description is brief, and the daughters and their prophetic gifts are not the main topic. However, by mentioning them, the author adds to Philip's stature. He is not only an evangelist himself but has family members who are highly regarded for their spiritual gifts.

One other example from Acts identifies a non-Christian woman with prophetic gifts. An event occurs while Paul and his companions were in Philippi, staying at Lydia's house.

> Once when we were going to the place of prayer, we were met by a
> female slave who had a spirit by which she predicted the future. She
> earned a great deal of money for her owners by fortune-telling. She
> followed Paul and the rest of us, shouting, "These men are servants
> of the Most High God, who are telling you the way to be saved."
> She kept this up for many days. Finally Paul became so annoyed
> that he turned round and said to the spirit, "In the name of Jesus
> Christ I command you to come out of her!" At that moment the
> spirit left her. (Acts 16:16–18)

Paul's actions anger the woman's owners, and they have Paul jailed.
But the encounter with her is interesting in its confirmation that prophetic gifts were common among non-Christians as well.

From the perspective of the storyteller, this woman's gifts aren't
quite on the up-and-up. For one thing, her owners are in this for the
money, not to spread the divine will. Their motivations are suspect.
And something about the woman annoys Paul, who exorcises the
spirit. Perhaps because of these clues, the English translators of the
NIV and other modern translations render the Greek in a way that
makes it seem like something other than prophecy. She has a "spirit
by which she predicts the future" and engages in "fortune-telling."
That's not a bad translation by any means, but it emphasizes the way
in which her gifts are suspect from Luke's perspective.

The words used in this passage would have signified prophetic
activity to readers of the time, however. The word translated "predicts
the future" means that the woman has a spirit associated with the god
Apollo—although she wasn't one of the "official" prophets at Apollo's
shrine at Delphi. And the word "fortune-telling" is an everyday
word for prophecy or consulting an oracle. This woman had a spirit
that allowed her to give oracles that were associated with the god
Apollo—a god from whom many people at the time would have liked
to hear. So, even if this isn't the most traditional form of prophecy,
many people at the time would recognize it as prophetic activity.

Even though people of the time would associate the woman with prophecy, many did not believe that this kind of prophecy was real. It wasn't just Christians who criticized the practice. For example, Plutarch agrees with the assessment in Acts that this mode of prophecy is suspect. And Plutarch had a strong connection to the shrine at Delphi, so he wasn't against devotion to Apollo. Nevertheless, he criticizes those who believe that the god, like a ventriloquist, "enters into the bodies of prophets and prompts their utterances."[3] That description fits how Acts describes this woman—or at least what some people must have believed about her.

Although the woman's owners are portrayed as charlatans, it's interesting that the woman's message nevertheless is pretty accurate. She says, "These men are servants of the Most High God, who are telling you the way to be saved" (Acts 16:17). That seems a pretty good summary of the situation! It may be a similar situation to what happens in Mark, when the demons recognize Jesus (e.g., Mark 1:23–28, 34). And, like Mark's Jesus, Paul exorcises this prophetic spirit, even if it is saying accurate things. For our purposes, the point is that the early readers of Acts would have understood the woman as someone participating in the culture of prophecy that was very familiar at the time.

There are fewer textual instances in which women are explicitly identified as praying. We've already seen two of them. Paul asserts that women who pray in church should cover their heads (1 Cor. 11:4–5). And the prophet Anna worshiped in the temple "with fasting and prayer night and day" (Luke 2:37). When Jesus arrived, "she began to give thanks to God"—a kind of prayer—and to speak of Jesus to those in the temple. Both Anna and women in Paul's churches are engaged in prayer.

Believers are regularly admonished to pray, and these instructions are, of course, directed toward both men and women. For example, when Jesus teaches "love your enemies and pray for those who persecute you" (Matt. 5:44), he certainly means female as well as male followers. Or when Ephesians admonishes us to take up the armor of God, praying "in the Spirit on all occasions" (Eph. 6:18), these instructions are for the whole church.

One further instance of prayer occurs after Peter's arrest by King Herod (Acts 12:1–5). During his imprisonment, "the church was earnestly praying to God for him" (12:5). Following Peter's miraculous release, "he went to the house of Mary the mother of John, also called Mark, where many had gathered and were praying" (12:12). No people are named specifically as praying, but the fact that Mary is the host of this gathering would make it more likely that she spoke.

Believers are regularly admonished to pray.

Explore these New Testament passages regarding the speech of women.

THE LUKAN BIRTH NARRATIVE

Two familiar portions of the birth narrative in Luke suggest the idea of women prophesying, although they are not called "prophets."

> At that time Mary got ready and hurried to a town in the hill country of Judea, where she entered Zechariah's home and greeted Elizabeth. When Elizabeth heard Mary's greeting, the baby leaped in her womb, and Elizabeth was filled with the Holy Spirit. In a loud voice she exclaimed: "Blessed are you among women, and blessed is the child you will bear! But why am I so favored, that the mother of my Lord should come to me? As soon as the sound of your greeting reached my ears, the baby in my womb leaped for joy. Blessed is she who has believed that the Lord would fulfil his promises to her!" (Luke 1:39–45)

1. Imagine yourself as an ancient reader who is familiar with women prophets. List the clues in this passage that suggest to you that Elizabeth prophesies.

Immediately after Elizabeth speaks, Mary begins:

> "My soul magnifies the Lord,
>   and my spirit rejoices in God my Savior,
> for he has been mindful of the humble estate of his servant.
>   From now on all generations will call me blessed;
> for the Mighty One has done great things for
>   me—holy is his name.
> His mercy extends to those who fear him,
>   from generation to generation.
> He has performed mighty deeds with his arm;
>   he has scattered those who are proud in their
>   inmost thoughts.
> He has brought down rulers from their thrones
>   but has lifted up the humble.
> He has filled the hungry with good things
>   but has sent the rich away empty.
> He has helped his servant Israel,
>   remembering to be merciful,
> to Abraham and his descendants for ever,
>   just as he promised our ancestors." (Luke 1:46–55)

2.   Again, imagine yourself as an ancient reader who is familiar with women prophets. List the clues in this passage that suggest to you that Mary's speech is prophetic.

PETER AT PENTECOST

Another familiar narrative—Peter preaching at Pentecost—interprets the pouring out of God's Spirit in relation to prophecy:

"These people are not drunk, as you suppose. It's only nine in the morning! No, this is what was spoken by the prophet Joel:

> 'In the last days, God says,
> I will pour out my Spirit on all people.
> Your sons and daughters will prophesy,
>   your young men will see visions,
>   your old men will dream dreams.
> Even on my servants, both men and women,
>   I will pour out my Spirit in those days,
>   and they will prophesy.'" (Acts 2:15–18)

Peter interprets the gift of the Spirit among Christians as a fulfillment of Joel's prophecy. What does this say to you about the roles of women in these communities?

14

Silence

Phoebe was a patron, a deacon, and Paul commended her. She lived in a culture in which women spoke for a lot of different reasons. But did she address the church in Rome? Many will answer no for one reason: their understanding that Paul did not allow women to speak.

We are accustomed to thinking that the main instruction to women about speaking is *not* to do it. For example, part of 1 Timothy reads: "A woman should learn in quietness and full submission. I do not permit a woman to teach or to assume authority over a man; she must be quiet" (1 Tim. 2:11–12). Would the expectation that women be quiet have restricted Phoebe's ability to speak?

In the previous two chapters, we've looked at social patterns that encouraged women's speech. But to understand the whole picture, we also need to consider what the norms were surrounding silence. So in this chapter and the next, we'll do precisely that. Was it the case that silence was a "rule" that women were to follow under every circumstance? Or was silence a rule that applied in some situations but not in others? These expectations would shape the way that Paul's readers understood Phoebe and her role.

Social norms regarding silence did indeed exist in the New Testament period, but they were considerably more flexible than we might expect. For one thing, there was variety in how the "rule of silence" was applied in different circumstances. If we can better understand what this rule meant to people of the time, we may be able to understand how it would have been applied in the early church. So let's look at the rule itself and what people thought was important about it. In the following chapter we'll consider how people in the culture applied the rule of silence in their everyday lives.

The Rule of Silence

The idea that women should be silent doesn't occur only in the New Testament. It was common advice at the time. Here are two examples of ancient male writers invoking norms of women's silence.

The philosopher Plutarch was aware of the ideals of women's silence. In a work titled *Advice to the Bride and Groom,* he wrote that women should let their husbands speak for their family: "A wife should speak only to her husband or through her husband, and should not feel aggrieved if, like a piper, she makes nobler music through another's tongue."[1] Plutarch is saying that women can speak to their husbands, but if they want to address a wider audience, they should let their husbands do the actual talking. The ideal is that husbands are the voice of the family and wives defer to them.

The second example is part of the story about the Roman women who protested laws restricting displays of wealth. The Senate was considering repealing the laws, and the women gathered in the streets around the Forum lobbying the senators as they gathered to debate. The main speaker against the women's position was a famous man named Cato, and he argued that the women's behavior was part of the reason the Senate should uphold these laws. He said, "What sort of practice is this, of running out into the streets and blocking the roads and speaking to other women's husbands? Could you not have made the same requests, each of your own husband, at home?"[2] Cato suggests that the women's behavior is

The idea that women should be silent was common advice.

inappropriate. They should only speak at home and to their husbands about the matter.

If Cato's words sound familiar, it may be because Paul's wording in 1 Corinthians 14:35 is similar to Cato's speech. Paul writes, "If they want to inquire about something, they should ask their own husbands at home." The similarities in all these sources have led many people to suggest there was a hard-and-fast rule forbidding women's speech. End of story, right? Well, maybe not. As we've already seen, women had many occasions to speak. If we understand a little more about what ancient people valued about silence, it may help us to see why these rules could be more malleable than they first appear.

What Silence Meant

In the New Testament period, silence was a virtue for any person who was in the presence of those society considered of higher social status. This was true of women when they were among men of higher status. But it was also true of men when they were in the presence of people of high standing.

Silence was an aspect of that important virtue that keeps cropping up everywhere: self-control. Philosophers considered control of one's tongue to be something very difficult! Speaking wisely meant knowing what to say, but it also meant knowing when to be silent. Many writers criticize the "babbler" who doesn't really have anything helpful to contribute but keeps on talking nonetheless. The self-controlled person refrained from speaking when it was not necessary, or when it was someone else's turn to speak.

Silence was a virtue for any person.

Consider the following quotation from the same philosopher, Plutarch: "It will be very advantageous for chatterers always to be in the company of their superiors and elders, out of respect for whose opinion they will become accustomed to silence."[3] This sounds like something we might expect to apply to women, but Plutarch was thinking of a *male* audience in this case. The "chatterers" he has in mind are men. Plutarch teaches that being in the presence of elders is good training for men to be able to keep silence when circumstances required it.

Because Roman society was very hierarchical, knowing to whom one could speak and what to say was very important, not just for women but for men as well. Plutarch considered it worthwhile for men to train themselves to keep silence when it was appropriate, which was in the presence of their superiors and elders. The same principle was true for women in the presence of men who were of higher social rank. It was a virtue to be silent in those cases.

Sometimes women were socially superior to men.

However, sometimes women were socially superior to men. It is important to keep in mind that not all women were inferior to all men. It can seem as if all women were beneath all men, because we have evidence of ancient people saying that, in general, women are inferior to men, and slaves are inferior to free people, and so forth. But in practice a person's status depended on a combination of factors. Gender was merely one thing that made up one's social status. Other important components were age, wealth, ancestry, enslaved or freeborn status, and citizenship. This led to a lot of variety that might surprise us!

For example, some slaves of the emperor were powerful people and would have been viewed as having higher social standing than a poor freeborn person. A woman might have higher status than a man who was of lower birth, or who had less money, or who was younger. A person with Roman citizenship would have higher standing than a citizen of, say, Ephesus, if other factors in their status were the same.

Being male or female was also an aspect of social status. If all other factors were equal, a man would have more standing than a woman, just because he was a man. We have often thought of gender as the one thing that trumped all others, but that really wasn't the case. A wealthy woman had higher status than most men.

Elite women clearly found themselves in many situations in which they were higher ranking than other men. But not all lower-class women were inferior to all men. Social status was always relative, and it depended on who was with you at any given time. If an elite man was in a room with his parents and their peers, his silence would show good breeding. And if a woman business owner was in her market stall with other vendors and customers, she might have higher status than the men involved.

Sometimes the social expectations were the reverse of what we expect, and a man was silent because of a woman's status. One story tells of a man who was traveling to another town when he encountered a wealthy aunt of his whom he didn't know very well. A slave encouraged him to speak to her, but he declined. He narrates the story this way: "'I am embarrassed in front of a woman whom I do not know,' I answered, suddenly blushing, and I just stood there looking at the ground. Then she turned and stared at me. 'He inherited that well-bred behavior,' she said, 'from his pure and virtuous mother, Salvia.'"[4] Here the male narrator's silence was interpreted as virtuous. He waited for his aunt to address him first, out of deference to her higher status.

Also complicating the question of who should speak is that people assessed the speaker's virtue in addition to the speaker's social standing. A highborn man could still be deemed a poor speaker in comparison to a freedman if the latter had studied philosophy and excelled in learning. Even though Roman society was very hierarchical, there was a considerable amount of social mobility in this period, and people acknowledged that demonstrating virtue was an important qualification.

So, in part, a person's speech was judged based on whether people found it to be wise or foolish. The women we've encountered who spoke bravely in times of disaster clearly felt they had permission to do so, or their stories would never have been told. But these stories were told and retold because the woman's speech or action was deemed to be wise.

And in those cases, a woman's speech was welcome. Recall the case of Judith from the previous chapter. She was a virtuous woman of high status in her village. She summoned the elders and criticized their actions. Her speech actually reinforced her virtue—in part because her assessment of the situation was correct. Even the elders against whom she spoke acknowledged her wisdom. Judith's status, both as a wealthy woman and as a virtuous person, made it more likely that her speech would be welcomed.

A woman's speech was welcome.

Silence was an important skill in ancient times. It conveyed deference to elders and other high-ranking people. If you could control your tongue, you were less likely to act in a way you'd regret later. And, aside from these practical benefits, silence was a virtue. Keeping quiet in the right circumstances conveyed wisdom and self-discipline.

Silence in the New Testament

The New Testament shares the value of controlling one's speech. It's not just women who should be silent; men should be as well. Here's an example from the letter of James about how it is difficult but necessary to curb one's speech: "All kinds of animals, birds, reptiles and sea creatures are being tamed and have been tamed by mankind, but no human being can tame the tongue. It is a restless evil, full of deadly poison. With the tongue we praise our Lord and Father, and with it we curse human beings, who have been made in God's likeness. Out of the same mouth come praise and cursing. My brothers and sisters, this should not be" (James 3:7–10). James teaches that speaking well is difficult *for everyone*. It's easy to get carried away and say things we should not. Thus, the ability to be silent is a virtue.

In 1 Timothy, silence was also framed as an act of self-control. First Timothy 2:9 says that women should "dress modestly, with decency and propriety." The word "propriety" is the same Greek word (*sōphrosynē*) that means self-control. This word occurs in both the first and last verses of 1 Timothy 2:9–15, so it seems to frame the subject of this passage. In the New Testament period, discussions of the virtue of self-control often included both dress and speech: one should not wear clothing that is too elaborate, and one should speak the right amount to the right people. Both of these topics occur in this passage, so the passage seems to share the conventional virtue of self-control.

The exhortation to silence reflected the gendered social norms of its time. The two New Testament passages that enjoined women to silence reflected the culture's presumption that women were generally considered to be of lower status than men. First Corinthians states that women "are not allowed to speak, but must be in submission" (14:34). Here, the prohibition against speech was articulated directly in relationship to women's subordinate status. Similarly, 1 Timothy asserts that a woman is not "to teach or to assume authority over a man; she must be quiet" (2:12). Silence represented recognition of the differential in cultural authority accorded to men and women.

The New Testament shares the value of controlling one's speech.

All of this would have been very familiar to early readers of 1 Timothy or 1 Corinthians. This was conventional, everyday wisdom. It was good to be silent before those who were honorable. Silence was an exercise in self-control. The passages in the New Testament that encourage silence affirm these important cultural values. Women were often encouraged to be quiet and let the men speak.

Modern interpreters often assert that the authors of these passages were responding to some sort of disturbance. Some women were teaching or speaking in ways that were disruptive, and so the writer advocated silence in order to counteract the problem. That's possible, of course; when we imagine a specific scenario for these letters, we are only speculating, so we'll never really know. But other authors of the time affirmed these principles *without* a pressing reason. They viewed silence as a difficult but important skill practiced by those who excelled in virtue. The New Testament authors—who affirm the importance of self-control in other places—may simply have agreed.

In the following passages, consider how the virtue of silence may be visible in passages of the New Testament that *aren't* specifically about women.

INSTRUCTIONS TO SPEAKERS

Paul gives instructions to various speakers in worship, not just women. Here's what he says:

> Everything must be done so that the church may be built up. If anyone speaks in a tongue, two—or at the most three—should speak, one at a time, and someone must interpret. If there is no interpreter, the speaker should keep quiet in the church and speak to himself and to God. Two or three prophets should speak, and the others should weigh carefully what is said. And if a revelation comes to someone who is sitting down, the first speaker should stop. For you can all prophesy in turn so that everyone may be instructed and encouraged. The spirits of prophets are subject to the control of prophets. For God is not a God of disorder but of peace—as in all the congregations of the Lord's people. (1 Cor. 14:26–33)

1. The word used in verse 28 that's translated "keep quiet" and the word in verse 30 that's translated "should stop" are the same Greek word. It's also the same Greek word as in 14:34: "Women should remain silent in the churches." Read verses 28 and 30 again and write down why the speakers are instructed to be silent. Include the specific wording that leads you to understand the reason for this instruction.

Verse 28

Verse 30

2. Do you think ancient readers of 1 Corinthians would have understood these instructions to be consistent with their understanding that silence was an expression of self-control? Explain your answer.

JESUS HEALS A BLIND MAN

Luke's Gospel includes a story of Jesus healing a blind man. It starts with the blind man calling out to Jesus and being shushed:

> As Jesus approached Jericho, a blind man was sitting by the roadside begging. When he heard the crowd going by, he asked what was happening. They told him, "Jesus of Nazareth is passing by." He called out, "Jesus, Son of David, have mercy on me!" Those who led the way rebuked him and told him to be quiet, but he shouted all the more, "Son of David, have mercy on me!" (Luke 18:35–39)

Why does the crowd tell the blind man to be silent? (To be clear, this is the same Greek word as above.) Draw on the social expectations about silence to give an explanation of the crowd's demand.

15

Speech and Silence

Phoebe knew her culture's expectations about silence, which we studied in the previous chapter. She knew that a person's silence was a virtue when it showed deference to someone of higher status. She knew that silence showed self-control, because it was difficult to be quiet when you had something to say. It's hard to imagine Phoebe attaining the status she had in the church without understanding these rules.

But how would those rules apply to Phoebe in her visit to Rome? To understand the New Testament period, we need to know the rules of culture, but we also need to be aware of how people of the time thought the rules should be applied. Silence wasn't a blanket rule— there were times when speech was appropriate, and times when silence was better. Cultural norms supply rules, but they also teach us how the rules apply in different situations.

Think about our own culture for a moment. In North American society, we value freedom of speech. It's an important right we have, that we can voice our political opinions without government interference. We don't choose to exercise that freedom in every situation, how- ever. For example, most of us would never stand up in the middle of a movie theater and start making a political speech. We remain silent in that situation, but it's not because at that moment we don't value our

Silence wasn't a blanket rule.

constitutional rights! Instead, culture teaches us that the rules have
to be applied in different ways in different situations.

So, even though it's fair to say there was a "rule of silence" in the
New Testament period, we should also think about how people within
that culture applied the rule. We've certainly seen plenty of evidence
that women's speech was not always viewed as breaking the rules.
How did the social norms shape women's speech and silence?

Applying the Rules of Culture

Let's think about the rule of silence as expressed by Plutarch and
Cato. Plutarch said women should only speak to their husbands and
should let their husbands speak for the family, but how did he understand that rule to be applied?

In the same book where he writes that women should only speak
to their husbands, Plutarch also quotes a number of women philosophers. He approves of various things these women had said, and he
uses their words to support his ideas. He also recommends a philosophical treatise that his wife had written. So Plutarch doesn't seem
to think that women should never make their voices known.

In his other writings, Plutarch tells stories of women whose speech
he approves of. We recall that Plutarch praises a woman named Chilonis, who appealed to her father in a highly charged political moment
to spare the life of her husband. The two had been political enemies,
and Chilonis spoke out in a large group of people to remind her father
that showing mercy would mean he was a good leader, not a tyrant.
Plutarch tells other stories where women of high standing spoke in
political situations to protect the safety of their people.

The point is that Plutarch knew about the social norms that said
women should defer to more powerful men in their speech. However,
when he applied them to real life, silence was not the only option
for women. There were many different scenarios in which a woman
might speak. Some were so commonplace that no one would even

bother to mention them. And other times women spoke in moments of political or familial crisis, and their words were welcomed as wise and appropriate. So it does not seem that the rule about silence that Plutarch cites was applied rigorously in every situation.

The same is true with the other example of the rule of silence we read in the last chapter. Cato made a speech opposing the repeal of some laws, but the women of the city protested for their removal. Cato said of the women: "Could you not have made the same requests, each of your own husband, at home?" Although this sounds as if Cato is telling the women directly to go home and be quiet, his words are part of political debate, so he's speaking to the other senators and not to the women at all! He quotes himself saying what he *could* have said to the women.

Cato speaks as if everyone knows that women should be silent, and he uses that idea as part of his argument. It was a common idea, after all, as we saw in the previous chapter. Cato used it to suggest that the women's actions were a kind of uncontrolled behavior that would only increase if the laws were repealed. But he didn't actually try to prevent the women from speaking.

Even more interesting is the reason why Cato says he stopped himself from saying these things to the women. He says he *could* have told the women to speak only to their husbands *but didn't* because some of them were dignified and modest. Cato invokes the social rule that women should not speak, but he also chooses to be silent himself rather than rebuke these high-standing women.

Another important thing is that Cato's opponent, Valerius, supports women's speech. I'll paraphrase his words because it's a long speech, but he basically says, "Hey, these women aren't doing anything new. Women have always spoken up about things that concern them. And by the way, Cato, in your own history book you wrote down a bunch of those stories praising women's speech, so don't pretend you don't think women should ever speak." By noting that Cato had also praised women's speech in some circumstances, Valerius undercuts the assertion that women should never speak on political matters. He retells stories that bring to mind familiar history in which women's speech was expected and even praiseworthy.

Cato's speech reminds us that there was an ideal of women's silence on which Cato could draw for his argument. But Valerius's argument also tells us something important about ancient ideals: he reminds his listeners that women's speech is not unusual. Indeed, it can be praised and upheld as an example of bravery and civic-mindedness.

In case you're wondering how it turned out, the women's side prevailed. The historian Livy says that the day after Cato and Valerius spoke, even more women came out to advocate for the repeal of the laws, and they convinced the leaders to allow the repeal. If women's silence had been a hard-and-fast rule, presumably the women's appeals would not have been successful!

Thus, when we describe the rules of speech and silence in the first century, we need to consider evidence that there were norms restricting women's speech, but that there were also conventions that encouraged women to speak. People agreed that it was better for women to be silent around men of higher status (which usually included their husbands), but that they should also speak up in support of their families' interests. In some circumstances, women were even praised for speaking boldly to men who had higher status than they did.

I would summarize the cultural "rules" about speech and silence this way:

1. Silence was evidence of virtue for men and women when it showed self-control in the presence of people with higher status.
2. Sometimes women were socially superior to men, and then they could be expected to speak.
3. Bold speech on behalf of a woman's city or family was virtuous.

These more nuanced rules help explain why we see the ideal of silence alongside so many instances of women speaking. The culture preferred men as speakers, especially when they had higher status than women. But the speech of women wasn't forbidden. Women's speech was especially valued when they spoke to secure the interests of their families or communities.

Silence and Speech in the New Testament

Like the culture at large, the New Testament exhibited evidence of women's speech *and* social norms of women's subordination and silence. Because of this similarity, first-century readers would have understood statements about women's silence as rules that they applied according to the conventions of their day. These readers were familiar with statements that women should be subordinate to men and with assumptions that they should not speak. It seems quite likely that they would have understood New Testament language about women's silence in this way.

Control of the tongue was a virtue that did not always demand complete silence, even of women. The virtue of silence is seen in New Testament texts, including those that assumed the leadership of women. We're used to hearing 1 Timothy's words about silence (1 Tim. 2:11-12). But in the next chapter of this letter, the qualifications for church leaders included self-control with regard to speech. A bishop was to be "able to teach" and "not quarrelsome" (3:2, 3). Male deacons likewise should be "sincere" (1 Tim. 3:8; more literally, "not insincere"). And similar qualifications applied to the female deacons, who should not be "malicious talkers" (3:11). False or duplicitous speaking is inappropriate to the life of faith and should disqualify men and women from leadership. The implication is that men and women both spoke, and that good leaders would include those who spoke truthfully.

The language of 1 Corinthians shows the same combination: a rule about silence alongside women who speak. Paul's statement that women "are not allowed to speak" (1 Cor. 14:34) reiterates the social norms we've seen. The cultural assumption was that a well-ordered community would prefer the speech of husbands over that of wives. But 1 Corinthians also discusses women's speech as a normal part of worship. Paul directs that women who pray or prophesy should cover their heads (11:5–6), while men should not. Paul moreover praises prophecy as a very important spiritual gift (12:28; 14:1), and he assumes that women have that gift and share it in the churches.

If "they are not allowed to speak" were the rule, it was still a rule that would be applied according to the norms of culture. Given the many situations in which the speech of women was also conventional, Paul would have needed to explain things in greater detail if he wanted to prohibit all speech by women—especially because he had already mentioned women's prayer and prophecy in a way that acknowledged their speech. Paul isn't contradicting himself: he's speaking in ways that readers at the time would have understood. When applied according to cultural norms, the "rule" of women's silence did not prohibit these forms of speech. Indeed, such speech was encouraged without being perceived as breaking the social norms.

The "rule" of women's silence did not prohibit these forms of speech.

Now it's time to summarize what you've seen about speech and silence in the New Testament.

SPEECH AND SILENCE IN THE NEW TESTAMENT

On the one hand, we have New Testament statements that instruct women to be silent. On the other hand, we have examples of women speaking for various reasons. We list them here. The examples of speech are the same ones you studied in chapters 10 and 11.

SILENCE

1 Corinthians 14:33–35	Women should be silent
1 Timothy 2:11–12	Women should be silent

SPEECH

Matthew 15:21–28	A Canaanite woman appeals to Jesus for her daughter
Matthew 20:20–23	The mother of the sons of Zebedee appeals for her sons' advancement
Matthew 27:19	The wife of Pilate reports a dream of Jesus's innocence
Mark 6:17–29	Herodias asks for (and receives) John the Baptist's head
Mark 14:66–69	A slave accuses Peter of being Jesus's disciple
Luke 2:36–38	Anna speaks in the temple about Jesus
Luke 18:1–8	A widow appeals to a judge for her interests
John 20:18	Mary Magdalene proclaims, "I have seen the Lord!"
Acts 16:15	Lydia prevails on Paul to stay with her
Acts 18:26	Priscilla and Aquila explain the Way of God to Apollos
Acts 21:9	Four daughters have the gift of prophecy

Describe the evidence that you see here. (You may want to return to these passages to remind yourself of the context.) Think about how the rules of culture applied in each situation. Use the space below to describe why you think the speech of these women was acceptable.

PASSAGE	*Why women's speech was acceptable*
Matthew 15:21–28	
Matthew 20:20–23	
Matthew 27:19	
Mark 6:17–29	
Mark 14:66–69	
Luke 2:36–38	
Luke 18:1–8	
John 20:18	
Acts 16:15	
Acts 18:26	
Acts 21:9	

REFLECTIONS

Reflect on what you've read about both speech and silence, and write your ideas in the space below.

PHOEBE AND 1 TIMOTHY 2:11–12

Many churches that restrict women's leadership nowadays draw heavily on 1 Timothy 2:11–12 to support their views. Some interpret these verses as a blanket prohibition of women's pastoral leadership, others as a restriction on women leading men or women preaching. How do you think a woman like Phoebe would have understood these verses?

Conclusion

Paul and Phoebe had a close and cooperative relationship. It's clear from what Paul says in Romans that he respects her a great deal. But he only gives us a tiny window into understanding who she was and what her role was in the church. Throughout this book, we've therefore drawn on historical information to understand what readers of the time would have assumed when they encountered Paul's brief mention of Phoebe. We can't fill in all the gaps—there's a lot we'll never know for sure—but we can make some educated guesses about the roles Phoebe played in her church in Cenchreae and on her visit to Rome.

Our goal hasn't simply been to understand Phoebe, as interesting as she is. We've been trying to think about the cultural norms that shaped the lives of all women in the New Testament period—both the characters we see and the many, many women followers whose names and stories we'll never know.

This concluding chapter asks you to think through what you've seen and learned in earlier chapters of this book. The goal all along has not been to give you a single answer describing what the New Testament says about women's leadership. Instead, the book has given a more accurate and broader historical picture that may allow you to think about the New Testament as its earliest readers might have understood it. The history is an important part of your tool kit for interpreting the New Testament well.

So now it's time to gather up your ideas and draw your own conclusions. This chapter is designed to help synthesize your thoughts on the basis of what you've seen in the previous chapters. There are three basic steps involved in this: (1) summarizing the historical picture, (2) deciding how this history shapes your understanding of women in the New Testament, and (3) deciding how this interpretation of the New Testament shapes your thoughts about women in ministry. The sections of the chapter give you space to articulate your thoughts on each of these topics.

Assessing the Historical Picture

Modern readers have long noticed the variety in evidence about women's roles in antiquity. Some evidence indicates that women were active contributors, not only to their own households but to the larger economic and social order. Their communities noted and appreciated their leadership. Other evidence states restrictions on women's actions or presents women as inferior to men.

Some resolve this apparent contradiction by saying that the evidence applies to different groups of women. For example, only elite women escaped the constraints of being female and held civic titles. Some historians of early Christianity have argued that only heretical groups had women leaders.

This book has offered a different explanation, in part because there are so many ancient sources that express both ideas simultaneously. We saw how Junia Theodora was both "modest" and an advocate for her people, for example. To the people of the time, these concepts weren't mutually exclusive.

I have argued that the social norms of the time were complex. Sometimes cultural norms were in tension. For example, social standing was important, and one way families displayed status was by wearing fancy clothes. At the same time, other norms said it was a virtue to dress simply, and that doing so displayed good judgment. Deciding what to wear wasn't an all-or-nothing proposition—as if some people must always wear all their fine jewelry and others none. Instead, these were values on which individuals drew as they made decisions, and the balance between them might shift depending on the circumstances.

Another way ancient social norms were complex was that there were different ways to enact them depending on the context. This is true for us as well. For example, we have social norms around modest dress—though they're less rigid than they used to be. These norms are different depending on the location. For example, it means one thing to dress modestly when you go to the beach, and another thing entirely to dress modestly when you go to church. What is more, it's hard to imagine that someone would confuse the two contexts

Social norms supported and even encouraged the social influence and economic participation of women.

and show up to church in a nice, modest bathing suit! That is because culture doesn't merely give us rules about modesty; it also gives us the knowledge we need to apply the rules to different circumstances.

The same was true of women in the New Testament period. A woman might decide not to speak up in a group of male peers—unless she felt the situation warranted her intervention. But she might also find herself in another group where she was among those of highest status, and in that case her speech might be welcomed and expected. She might defer to a male patron but also be honored for her leadership in a civic organization.

This complexity helps us understand how women played different roles but were still praised for traditional virtues. A woman like Junia Theodora advocated politically for her community and was characterized as "living modestly." Amymone was idealized as "devoted to her home," even though her everyday pursuit of her family's well-being probably took her away from her house. The evidence suggests that society did not view such women as abandoning traditional virtues.

There were social norms that supported and even encouraged the social influence and economic participation of women.

1. Use the categories below to list the kinds of evidence you have seen. Go back through the chapters and collect the evidence that's relevant for each idea. It may take some time to put the pieces together, but in doing so you'll be thinking through what's important for your understanding of the subject.

    A. Ancient readers were familiar with a variety of forms of leadership by women.

    B. There were traditional, gendered norms that shaped women's behavior.

    C. Women's leadership and feminine virtues went hand in hand.

2. Go back to the end of the introduction and look at what you wrote in response to question 4 (on p. 7). The question asked whether anything in the inscription honoring Junia Rustica surprised you or contradicted your ideas about ancient women. Now you're in a position to say whether you've seen other evidence that confirmed that what

you saw in the inscription was more generally true of women in the period. Use this space to record your ideas now that you're at the end of the study.

Interpreting the New Testament

How might this historical background affect the way we understand New Testament texts? Early readers of New Testament texts recognized a variety of everyday expectations for women's behavior. Modesty, industry, and loyalty were standard feminine virtues, yet they could be expressed in multiple ways. Furthermore, the virtues often went hand in hand with women's active pursuit of social, economic, and religious interests. Readers of the period came to the New Testament texts with this understanding already in place and read these passages in light of that cultural context.

1. How does the historical information you collected above affect your understanding of the New Testament?

    A. Brainstorm a list of passages of Scripture in which you think this historical background is important. (If you're working with a study group, this might be a great thing to do together.) You can list passages that were included in earlier chapters, and you can add stories that were not addressed directly.

B. How does the historical background help you to understand each passage? Do any familiar interpretations of these passages now seem unlikely to you, given what you now know about the historical context?

C. Which of the above passages are most important to you or your church community when you ask questions about women's leadership?

D. Reread the verses about Phoebe in Romans 16:1–2: "I commend to you our sister Phoebe, a deacon of the church in Cenchreae. I ask you to receive her in the Lord in a way worthy of his people and to give her any help she may need from you, for she has been the benefactor of many people, including me."

Based on what you have learned, what kind of a person do you think Phoebe was? Brainstorm a list of possible ways ancient readers might have understood Phoebe and her role.

2. What questions or issues haven't been addressed? This is a historical book, so it's limited to those kinds of questions. There may be

other related topics you want to explore. Or you may have additional questions about this historical period that you want to research. List those things here.

3. What kind of conclusions do you now draw about women in the New Testament?

Thinking about Women in Ministry Today

Many readers of this book already have firm ideas about the roles women should play in ministry in their congregations. Although you now have some new historical information, that doesn't necessarily mean you've changed your mind about this question. However, you may have some new ways of expressing your ideas about women in ministry.

1. What other factors influence the way you think about this topic today? Many Christians consider a number of things in addition to the biblical texts. Check off any of these that are important to you:

- The role of the Holy Spirit in calling people to ministry
- Social roles today that shape the role of the minister
- The weight of tradition
- The idea that the church should change over time in response to new situations

Add anything else that you think is important:

2. How does your understanding of the New Testament contribute to your understanding of women in ministry today?

Conclusion

My argument in this book has not been that the ancient church was egalitarian. It wasn't. Many passages of the New Testament communicate the commonly accepted idea that women were inferior to men. However, alongside these norms were other ideals that allowed and even encouraged women's active participation in their communities. And the New Testament texts conveyed those ideals as well.

Women who fulfilled the traditional feminine virtues often acted in ways that would surprise us, taking on roles as patrons and advocates, and serving in a variety of civic and religious offices. Early readers of the New Testament would have been familiar with women like Turia, who advocated for her family's needs before the city's ruler, or Junia Theodora, who was a patron and protector of her people. Both women were praised for modesty and for civic engagement. Modesty was a virtue that often went hand in hand with women's active pursuit of social, economic, and religious interests.

The church encouraged Christ-believing women to exhibit virtues that were widely acknowledged within the culture. The author of Titus expected the older women to teach the younger ones "to love their husbands and children, to be self-controlled and pure, to be busy at home, to be kind, and to be subject to their husbands, so that no one will malign the word of God" (Titus 2:4–5). For the first readers, who shared the social norms of the first and second centuries, these words may not have suggested the picture of docility that modern readers often expect. Readers of the letter to Titus may have understood women like Turia or Junia Theodora to exemplify this same model of virtue. Feminine virtues also described women who used their influence and resources in powerful ways to benefit their families and communities. Like them, the Christian women who displayed these virtues may also have been called upon to lead their communities in various ways.

The Christian women who displayed these virtues may also have been called upon to lead their communities in various ways.

Abbreviations

BGU	*Aegyptische Urkunden aus den Königlichen*
Bull. Epi.	*Bulletin épigraphique*
CIG	*Corpus Inscriptionum Graecarum*
CIJ	*Corpus Inscriptionum Judaicarum*
CIL	*Corpus Inscriptionum Latinarum*
ILS	*Inscriptiones Latinae Selectae*
P.Fay.	*Fayum Towns and Their Papyri*
P.Giss.	*Griechische Papyri zu Giessen*
P.Grenf.	*New Classical Fragments and Other Greek and Latin Papyri*
P.Kron.	*L'Archivio di Kronion*
Pleket	*Epigraphica II: Texts on the Social History of the Greek World*
P.Mich.	*Michigan Papyri*
P.Mil.Vogl.	*Papiri della R. Università di Milano*
P.Oxy.	*Oxyrynchus Papyri*
PSI	*Papiri greci e latini*
P.Yadin	*The Documents from the Bar Kochba Period in the Cave of Letters*
SB	*Sammelbuch griechischer Urkunden aus Aegypten*
SEG	*Supplementum Epigraphicum Graecum*
Stud.Pal.	*Studien zur Palaeographie und Papyruskunde*

Notes

Introduction

1. Unless otherwise indicated, quotations from Scripture come from the New International Version 2011.
2. *CIL* 2.1956. Translations are mine unless indicated otherwise.

Chapter 1

1. *BGU* 4.1103, trans. Rowlandson.
2. All quotations from the Apocrypha come from the New Revised Standard Version.

Chapter 2

1. *CIL* 10.5183.
2. Pliny the Younger, *Letters* 7.24.
3. *P.Grenf.* 2.45a, trans. Rowlandson.
4. *CIJ* 741.
5. Columella, *On Agriculture* 12.1–4.
6. *P.Mil.Vogl.* 2.77, trans. Bagnall and Cribiore.

Chapter 3

1. *P.Mich.* 2.121.recto, trans. Evans Grubbs.
2. *P.Yadin* 17, trans. Kraemer.
3. *Bull. Epi.* 1956, no. 213.
4. *BGU* 4.1103, trans. Rowlandson.
5. *BGU* 4.1105, trans. Rowlandson.
6. Philo, *De specialibus legibus* 3.30.

Chapter 4

1. *P.Mich.* 8.464, trans. Bagnall and Cribiore.
2. *P.Oxy.* 6.932, trans. Rowlandson.
3. *CIL* 4.1136.
4. *CIL* 6.7581, trans. Lefkowitz and Fant.
5. *CIG* 6855.G.

Chapter 5

1. *P.Kron.* 17.
2. *Pleket* 11.G, trans. Lefkowitz and Fant.
3. *CIJ* 1.811.
4. *CIL* 4.171, trans. Lefkowitz and Fant.

Chapter 6

1. Dio Cassius, *Roman History* 57.12, trans. Cary.
2. *SEG* 18.143.

Chapter 7

1. *Stud.Pal.* 22.40, trans. Rowlandson.
2. *P.Giss.* 80, trans. Rowlandson.

3. *PSI* 1.64, trans. Rowlandson.

4. *SB* 5.7572, trans. Bagnall and Cribiore.

Chapter 8

1. *CIL* 6.1527, 31670, trans. Shelton.

2. *CIL* 6.10230, trans. Lefkowitz and Fant.

3. Plutarch, *Advice to the Bride and Groom* 26, trans. Russell.

4. Plutarch, *Advice to the Bride and Groom* 7, trans. Russell.

5. Plutarch, *Advice to the Bride and Groom* 26, trans. Russell.

Chapter 9

1. *ILS* 8402.

Chapter 10

1. *CIL* 6.10230.

2. *CIL* 6.1527, 31670.

3. *CIL* 6.1527, 31670, trans. Shelton.

4. Plutarch, *The Virtues of Women* 26, trans. Babbitt.

5. Plutarch, *The Virtues of Women* 27, trans. Babbitt.

Chapter 11

1. Plutarch, *Advice to the Bride and Groom* 33, trans. Russell.

2. *BGU* 4.1105, trans. Rowlandson.

3. *CIL* 6.7581, trans. Lefkowitz and Fant.

4. Plutarch, *Advice to the Bride and Groom* 33, trans. Russell.

Chapter 12

1. *CIL* 6.9683.

2. Juvenal, *Satires* 6.437–442, trans. Braund.

3. *P.Mich.* 8.464, APIS translation.

4. *P.Fay.* 127, trans. Bagnall and Cribiore.

5. Livy, *History of Rome* 34.1–8, trans. Yardley.

Chapter 13

1. Xenophon, *Ephesian Tale* 5.4, trans. Henderson.

2. Xenophon, *Ephesian Tale* 5.11, trans. Henderson.

3. Plutarch, *On the Obsolescence of Oracles* 9, trans. Babbitt.

Chapter 14

1. Plutarch, *Advice to the Bride and Groom* 32, trans. Russell.

2. Livy, *History of Rome* 34.2.8–11, trans. Sage.

3. Plutarch, *On Talkativeness* 23, trans. Helmbold.

4. Apuleius, *Metamorphoses* 2.2, trans. Hanson.

For Further Reading

Throughout this book I have quoted many of the ancient sources from collections that make these sources available in English. I list them here, along with a few other selected works, for readers who would like to learn more. The ancient literary sources not listed here can be found in the Loeb Classical Library, https://www.loeb classics.com.

Bagnall, Roger S., and Raffaella Cribiore. *Women's Letters from Ancient Egypt: 300 BC–AD 800*. Ann Arbor: University of Michigan Press, 2006.

Grubbs, Judith Evans. *Women and the Law in the Roman Empire: A Sourcebook on Marriage, Divorce, and Widowhood*. New York: Routledge, 2002.

Hylen, Susan E. *Women in the New Testament World*. Oxford: Oxford University Press, 2018.

Kraemer, Ross Shepard. *Women's Religions in the Greco-Roman World*. Oxford: Oxford University Press, 2004.

Lefkowitz, Mary R., and Maureen B. Fant. *Women's Life in Greece and Rome: A Source Book in Translation*. 3rd ed. Baltimore: Johns Hopkins University Press, 2005.

Madigan, Kevin, and Carolyn Osiek. *Ordained Women in the Early Church: A Documentary History*. Baltimore: Johns Hopkins University Press, 2005.

Plutarch. "Advice to the Bride and Groom." In *Plutarch's "Advice to the Bride and Groom" and "A Consolation to His Wife": English Translations, Commentary, Interpretive Essays, and Bibliography*, edited by Sarah B. Pomeroy, 5–13. New York: Oxford University Press, 1999.

Rowlandson, Jane, ed. *Women and Society in Greek and Roman Egypt: A Sourcebook*. Cambridge: Cambridge University Press, 1998.

Shelton, Jo-Ann. *As the Romans Did: A Sourcebook in Roman Social History*. Oxford: Oxford University Press, 1998.

Index of Subjects

Index of Scripture and Other Ancient Sources